Yuval Dror
Editor

Innovative Approaches in Working with Children and Youth: New Lessons from the Kibbutz

Innovative Approaches in Working with Children and Youth: New Lessons from the Kibbutz has been co-published simultaneously as *Child & Youth Services*, Volume 22, Numbers 1/2 2001.

Pre-publication
REVIEWS,
COMMENTARIES,
EVALUATIONS . . .

"EXCELLENT. . . . OFFERS RICH DESCRIPTIONS of Israel's varied and sustained efforts to use the educational and social life of the kibbutz to supply emotional and intellectual support for youngsters with a variety of special needs. An excellent supplement to any education course that explores approaches to serving disadvantaged children at risk of failing both academically and in terms of becoming contributing members of society."

Steve Jacobson, PhD
Professor, Department of Educational
Leadership and Policy,
University of Buffalo, New York

The Haworth Press, Inc.

Innovative Approaches
in Working with Children
and Youth:
New Lessons from the Kibbutz

Innovative Approaches in Working with Children and Youth: New Lessons from the Kibbutz has been co-published simultaneously as *Child & Youth Services,* Volume 22, Numbers 1/2 2001.

The *Child & Youth Services*™ Monographic "Separates"

Below is a list of "separates," which in serials librarianship means a special issue simultaneously published as a special journal issue or double-issue *and* as a "separate" hardbound monograph. (This is a format which we also call a "DocuSerial.")

"Separates" are published because specialized libraries or professionals may wish to purchase a specific thematic issue by itself in a format which can be separately cataloged and shelved, as opposed to purchasing the journal on an on-going basis. Faculty members may also more easily consider a "separate" for classroom adoption.

"Separates" are carefully classified separately with the major book jobbers so that the journal tie-in can be noted on new book order slips to avoid duplicate purchasing.

You may wish to visit Haworth's website at . . .

http://www.HaworthPress.com

. . . to search our online catalog for complete tables of contents of these separates and related publications.

You may also call 1-800-HAWORTH (outside US/Canada: 607-722-5857), or Fax 1-800-895-0582 (outside US/Canada: 607-771-0012), or e-mail at:

getinfo@haworthpressinc.com

Innovative Approaches in Working with Children and Youth: New Lessons from the Kibbutz, edited by Yuval Dror (Vol. 22, No. 1/2, 2001). *"EXCELLENT. . . . OFFERS RICH DESCRIPTIONS of Israel's varied and sustained efforts to use the educational and social life of the kibbutz to supply emotional and intellectual support for youngsters with a variety of special needs. An excellent supplement to any education course that explores approaches to serving disadvantaged children at risk of failing both academically and in terms of becoming contributing members of society." (Steve Jacobson, PhD, Professor, Department of Educational Leadership and Policy, University of Buffalo, New York)*

Working with Children on the Streets of Brazil: Politics and Practice, Walter de Oliveira, PhD (Vol. 21, No. 1/2, 2000). *Working with Children on the Streets of Brazil is both a scholarly work on the phenomenon of homeless children and a rousing call to action that will remind you of the reasons you chose to work in social services.*

Intergenerational Programs: Understanding What We Have Created, Valerie S. Kuehne, PhD (Vol. 19, No. 2, 1999).

Caring on the Streets: A Study of Detached Youthworkers, Jacquelyn Kay Thompson (Vol. 19, No. 2, 1999).

Boarding Schools at the Crossroads of Change: The Influence of Residential Education Institutions on National and Societal Development, Yitzhak Kashti (Vol. 19, No. 1, 1998). *"This book is an essential, applicable historical reference for those interested in positively molding the social future of the world's troubled youth." (Juvenile and Family Court Journal)*

The Occupational Experience of Residential Child and Youth Care Workers: Caring and Its Discontents, edited by Mordecai Arieli, PhD (Vol. 18, No. 2, 1997). *"Introduces the social reality of residential child and youth care as viewed by care workers, examining the problem of tension between workers and residents and how workers cope with stress." (Book News, Inc.)*

The Anthropology of Child and Youth Care Work, edited by Rivka A. Eisikovits, PhD (Vol. 18, No. 1, 1996). *"A fascinating combination of rich ethnographies from the occupational field of residential child and youth care and the challenging social paradigm of cultural perspective." (Mordecai Arieli, PhD, Senior Teacher, Educational Policy and Organization Department, Tel-Aviv University, Israel)*

Travels in the Trench Between Child Welfare Theory and Practice: A Case Study of Failed Promises and Prospects for Renewal, George Thomas, PhD, MSW (Vol. 17, No. 1/2, 1994). *"Thomas musters enough research and common sense to blow any proponent out of the water. . . . Here is a person of real integrity, speaking the sort of truth that makes self-serving administrators and governments quail." (Australian New Zealand Journal of Family Therapy)*

Negotiating Positive Identity in a Group Care Community: Reclaiming Uprooted Youth, Zvi Levy (Vol. 16, No. 2, 1993). *"This book will interest theoreticians, practitioners, and policymakers in* *child and youth care, teachers, and rehabilitation counselors. Recommended for academic and health science center library collections." (Academic Library Book Review)*

Information Systems in Child, Youth, and Family Agencies: Planning, Implementation, and Service Enhancement, edited by Anthony J. Grasso, DSW, and Irwin Epstein, PhD (Vol. 16, No. 1, 1993). *"Valuable to anyone interested in the design and the implementation of a Management Information System (MIS) in a social service agency. . ." (John G. Orme, PhD, Associate Professor, College of Social Work, University of Tennessee)*

Assessing Child Maltreatment Reports: The Problem of False Allegations, edited by Michael Robin, MPH, ACSW (Vol. 15, No. 2, 1991). *"A thoughtful contribution to the public debate about how to fix the beleaguered system . . . It should also be required reading in courses in child welfare." (Science Books & Films)*

People Care in Institutions: A Conceptual Schema and Its Application, edited by Yochanan Wozner, DSW (Vol. 14, No. 2, 1990). *"Provides ample information by which the effectiveness of internats and the life of staff and internees can be improved." (Residential Treatment for Children & Youth)*

Being in Child Care: A Journey Into Self, edited by Gerry Fewster, PhD (Vol. 14, No. 2, 1990). *"Evocative and provocative. Reading this absolutely compelling work provides a transformational experience in which one finds oneself alternately joyful, angry, puzzled, illuminated, warmed, chilled." (Karen VanderVen, PhD, Professor, Program in Child Development and Child Care, School of Social Work, University of Pittsburgh)*

Homeless Children: The Watchers and the Waiters, edited by Nancy Boxill, PhD (Vol. 14, No. 1, 1990). *"Fill[s] a gap in the popular and professional literature on homelessness . . . . Policymakers, program developers, and social welfare practitioners will find it particulary useful." (Science Books & Films)*

Perspectives in Professional Child and Youth Care, edited by James P. Anglin, MSW, Carey J. Denholm, PhD, Roy V. Ferguson, PhD, and Alan R. Pence, PhD (Vol. 13, No. 1/2, 1990). *"Reinforced by empirical research and clear conceptual thinking, as well as the recognition of the relevance of personal transformation in understanding quality care." (Virginia Child Protection Newsletter)*

Specialist Foster Family Care: A Normalizing Experience, edited by Burt Galaway, PhD, MS, and Joe Hudson, PhD, MSW (Vol. 12, No. 1/2, 1989). *"A useful and practical book for policymakers and professionals interested in learning about the benefits of treatment foster care." (Ira M. Schwartz, MSW, Professor and Director, Center for the Study of Youth Policy, The University of Michigan School of Social Work)*

Helping the Youthful Offender: Individual and Group Therapies That Work, William B. Lewis, PhD (Vol. 11, No. 2, 1991). *"In a reader-friendly and often humorous style, Lewis explains the multilevel approach that he deems necessary for effective treatment of delinquents within an institutional context." (Criminal Justice Review)*

Family Perspectives in Child and Youth Services, edited by David H. Olson, PhD (Vol. 11, No. 1, 1989). *"An excellent diagnostic tool to use with families and an excellent training tool for our family therapy students. . . . It also offers an excellent model for parent training." (Peter Maynard, PhD, Department of Human Development, University of Rhode Island)*

Transitioning Exceptional Children and Youth into the Community: Research and Practice, edited by Ennio Cipani, PhD (Vol. 10, No. 2, 1989). *"Excellent set of chapters. A very fine contribution to the literature. Excellent text." (T. F. McLaughlin, PhD, Department of Special Education, Gonzaga University)*

Assaultive Youth: Responding to Physical Assaultiveness in Residential, Community, and Health Care Settings, edited by Joel Kupfersmid, PhD, and Roberta Monkman, PhD (Vol. 10, No. 1,

1988). *"At last here is a book written by professionals who do direct care with assaultive youth and can give practical advice." (Vicki L. Agee, PhD, Director of Correctional Services, New Life Youth Services, Lantana, Florida)*

Developmental Group Care of Children and Youth: Concepts and Practice, Henry W. Maier, PhD (Vol. 9, No. 2, 1988). *"An excellent guide for those who plan to devote their professional careers to the group care of children and adolescents." (Journal of Developmental and Behavioral Pediatrics)*

The Black Adolescent Parent, edited by Stanley F. Battle, PhD, MPH (Vol. 9, No. 1, 1987). *"A sound and insightful perspective on black adolescent sexuality and parenting." (Child Welfare)*

Qualitative Research and Evaluation in Group Care, edited by Rivka A. Eisikovits, PhD, and Yitzhak Kashti, PhD (Vol. 8, No. 3/4, 1987). *"Well worth reading. . . . should be read by any nurse involved in formally evaluating her care setting." (Nursing Times)*

Helping Delinquents Change: A Treatment Manual of Social Learning Approaches, Jerome S. Stumphauzer, PhD (Vol. 8, No. 1/2, 1986). *"'The best I have seen in the juvenile and criminal justice field in the past 46 years. It is pragmatic and creative in its recommended treatment approaches, on target concerning the many aspects of juvenile handling that have failed, and quite honest in assessing and advocating which practices seem to be working reasonably well." (Corrections Today)*

Residential Group Care in Community Context: Insights from the Israeli Experience, edited by Zvi Eisikovits, PhD, and Jerome Beker, EdD (Vol. 7, No. 3/4, 1986). *A variety of highly effective group care settings in Israel are examined, with suggestions for improving care in the United States.*

Adolescents, Literature, and Work with Youth, edited by J. Pamela Weiner, MPH, and Ruth M. Stein, PhD (Vol. 7, No. 1/2, 1985). *"A variety of thought-provoking ways of looking at adolescent literature." (Harvard Educational Review)*

Young Girls: A Portrait of Adolescence Reprint Edition, Gisela Konopka, DSW (Vol. 6, No. 3/4, 1985). *"A sensitive affirmation of today's young women and a clear recognition of the complex adjustments they face in contemporary society." (School Counselor)*

Adolescent Substance Abuse: A Guide to Prevention and Treatment, edited by Richard E. Isralowitz and Mark Singer (Vol. 6, No. 1/2, 1983). *''A valuable tool for those working with adolescent substance misusers.'' (Journal of Studies on Alcohol)*

Social Skills Training for Children and Youth, edited by Craig LeCroy, MSW (Vol. 5, No. 3/4, 1983). *"Easy to read and pertinent to occupational therapists." (New Zealand Journal of Occupational Therapy)*

Legal Reforms Affecting Child and Youth Services, edited by Gary B. Melton, PhD (Vol. 5, No. 1/2, 1983). *"A consistently impressive book. The authors bring a wealth of empirical data and creative legal analyses to bear on one of the most important topics in psychology and law." (John Monahan, School of Law, University of Virginia)*

Youth Participation and Experiential Education, edited by Daniel Conrad and Diane Hedin (Vol. 4, No. 3/4, 1982). *A useful introduction and overview of the current and possible future impact of experiential education on adolescents.*

Institutional Abuse of Children and Youth, edited by Ranae Hanson (Vol. 4, No. 1/2, 1982). *"Well researched . . . should be required reading for every school administrator, school board member, teacher, and parent." (American Psychological Association Division 37 Newsletter)*

Innovative Approaches in Working with Children and Youth: New Lessons from the Kibbutz

Yuval Dror
Editor

Innovative Approaches in Working with Children and Youth: New Lessons from the Kibbutz has been co-published simultaneously as *Child & Youth Services*, Volume 22, Numbers 1/2 2001.

The Haworth Press, Inc.
New York • London • Oxford

Innovative Approaches in Working with Children and Youth: New Lessons from the Kibbutz has been co-published simultaneously as *Child & Youth Services*™, Volume 22, Numbers 1/2 2001.

The Haworth Press, Inc., 10 Alice Street, Binghamton, NY 13904-1580 USA

Cover design by Thomas J. Mayshock Jr.

Library of Congress Cataloging-in-Publication Data

Innovative approaches in working with children and youth : new lessons from the kibbutz / Yuval Dror, editor.
    p. cm.
"Co-published simultaneously as Child & youth services, volume 22, numbers 1/2 2001."
Includes bibliographical references and index.
    ISBN 0-7890-1419-X (hard : alk. paper) – ISBN 0-7890-1420-3 (pbk. : alk. paper)
    1. Collective education–Israel. 2. Community education–Israel. 3. Educational innovations–Israel. I. Dror, Yuval. II. Child & youth services.
LC1027.I75 I55 2001
371.19′095964–dc21

2001051726

Indexing, Abstracting & Website/Internet Coverage

This section provides you with a list of major indexing & abstracting services. That is to say, each service began covering this periodical during the year noted in the right column. Most Websites which are listed below have indicated that they will either post, disseminate, compile, archive, cite or alert their own Website users with research-based content from this work. (This list is as current as the copyright date of this publication.)

Abstracting, Website/Indexing Coverage . . . . Year When Coverage Began

- **BUBL Information Service, An Internet-based Information Service for the UK higher education community <URL: http://bubl.ac.uk/>**. **1997**

- **Child Development Abstracts & Bibliography (in print & online)** **1982**

- **CINAHL (Cumulative Index to Nursing & Allied Health Literature) in print, EBSCO, and SilverPlatter, Data-Star, and PaperChase. (Support materials include Subject Heading List, Database Search Guide, and instructional video)** **1997**

- **CNPIEC Reference Guide: Chinese National Directory of Foreign Periodicals** **1997**

- **Criminal Justice Abstracts** **1982**

- **ERIC Clearinghouse on Elementary & Early Childhood Education**. **1982**

- **Exceptional Child Education Resources (ECER), (CD/ROM from SilverPlatter and hard copy)** **1982**

- **e-psyche, LLC <www.e-psyche.net>** **2001**

(continued)

*Special Bibliographic Notes related to special journal issues
(separates) and indexing/abstracting:*

- indexing/abstracting services in this list will also cover material in any "separate" that is co-published simultaneously with Haworth's special thematic journal issue or DocuSerial. Indexing/abstracting usually covers material at the article/chapter level.
- monographic co-editions are intended for either non-subscribers or libraries which intend to purchase a second copy for their circulating collections.
- monographic co-editions are reported to all jobbers/wholesalers/approval plans. The source journal is listed as the "series" to assist the prevention of duplicate purchasing in the same manner utilized for books-in-series.
- to facilitate user/access services all indexing/abstracting services are encouraged to utilize the co-indexing entry note indicated at the bottom of the first page of each article/chapter/contribution.
- this is intended to assist a library user of any reference tool (whether print, electronic, online, or CD-ROM) to locate the monographic version if the library has purchased this version but not a subscription to the source journal.
- individual articles/chapters in any Haworth publication are also available through the Haworth Document Delivery Service (HDDS).

Innovative Approaches in Working with Children and Youth: New Lessons from the Kibbutz

CONTENTS

ABOUT THE EDITOR

Yuval Dror is Associate Professor in the School of Education, Tel-Aviv University. He was Senior Lecturer and Head of Oranim, The School of Education of the Kibbutz Movement and Haifa University. His areas of specialization are the history of education (and social-moral education) in Eretz-Israel (pre-statehood) under the British Mandate, progressive education (including kibbutz education), and the development of special methodology in the history of education.

Professor Dror is a member of ISCHE (International Standing Conference for the History of Education), and the national associations for the History of Education in England and Canada; he is the secretary of the Israeli Association for the History of Education. He authored 80 articles and book chapters and is the editor of four books and "special issues" on kibbutz education. He is also the author or co-author of five books: *The Social-Moral Education of the Labor Movement Trend During the British Mandate in Pre-State Israel 1921-1948*, *Curricula in der Schule–Israel* (with Yaacov Lieberman), *The Professional School at the University Between Academia and the Field: The Haifa University School of Education 1963-1983*, *Jewish Education in the Years of the National Homeland* (with Shimon Reshef), and *The History of Kibbutz Education–Practice into Theory*.

Introduction

The purpose of this special volume is to bring to the international audiences of education and youthwork an update on the "state of the art" of child and youth services in the Israeli kibbutz and to describe what this audience can learn from this unique social and educational laboratory. This volume deals with "Innovative Approaches in Working with Children and Youth: New Lessons from the Kibbutz."

Since the mid-1980s, the kibbutz movement has experienced a deep social and economic crisis, but despite this negative influence on the semi-private kibbutz educational system, the uniqueness of "communal/cooperative education" has been maintained, and it even grew. The openness of the kibbutz to its neighbors from non-kibbutz settlements in the 1980s and 1990s enabled rural areas to succeed in fruitful cooperation with the kibbutz. These experiences are detailed in this volume.

In order to describe the innovations that are included in this special collection we shall start with the unique principles of kibbutz education theory. They are "historical" as well as contemporary; they are the product of a combination of the four main sources of kibbutz education (Zionist-Socialism, new/progressive education, the youth movement system, and psychoanalysis) into varied, practical educational methods that can be applied, in principle, beyond the kibbutz and Israel. These principles are:

1. The individual and social education of the child and the youth are at the center. Non-selective kibbutz education, which is responsible for every child until the 12th grade, is a model of educational integration of kibbutz-born individuals with both learning and other difficulties and with groups from outside the kibbutz. Sixty

[Haworth co-indexing entry note]: "Introduction." Dror, Yuval. Co-published simultaneously in *Child & Youth Services* (The Haworth Press, Inc.) Vol. 22, No. 1/2, 2001, pp. 1-5; and: *Innovative Approaches in Working with Children and Youth: New Lessons from the Kibbutz* (ed: Yuval Dror) The Haworth Press, Inc., 2001, pp. 1-5. Single or multiple copies of this article are available for a fee from The Haworth Document Delivery Service [1-800-342-9678, 9:00 a.m. - 5:00 p.m. (EST). E-mail address: getinfo@haworthpressinc.com].

1

thousand students of *Aliyat Hanoar* (Youth Aliyah immigration) were educated in the kibbutz, for example.

2. An educating society and environment that includes a two-way connection between kibbutz education and the surrounding area. The kibbutz is, by definition, an "ideal type" of "community education" rooted in the local and regional area and the same time in Israeli, Jewish, and international communities.
3. Integration of educational influences. The daily connection between the family and the "external" community has been permanently changed in many places, but these have always been retained in kibbutz education. The different models of cooperation and division of educational work can be learned by non-kibbutz societies, because connections between the family, the school, and the other educational factors are a central issue in any educational system.
4. Integration of community, academics, and work. The different forms of "work education" in the kibbutz, built into the curricula from kindergarten to high school, are relevant to "career education," "transitions between the world of studies and the world of work," and other vocational emphases.
5. Active learning, informal methods, and interdisciplinary approaches. Many progressive and non-formal methods were developed during the 90 years of kibbutz education, and this rich experience is meaningful from the didactic point of view.
6. Student autonomy in the children's society. This method of progressive institutions, as they are known in Europe and America, was practiced in the kibbutz in varied local, regional, and national frameworks. In the 1970s and 1980s, Kohlberg and his successors studied the children's society in the Anne Frank Haven at kibbutz Sasa: A secondary school based on full integration between kibbutz-born and city born (Youth Aliyah) children, the latter from lower socioeconomic backgrounds (Dror, 1995). He founded his "Just Community" approach according to the model of the direct democracy in Sasa (Kohlberg, 1985).
7. Autonomy of the educational staff. Kibbutz teachers followed their own "School Based Curriculum Development" from the 1920s, decades before this term was even known in the curriculum literature as "whole school curriculum planning" or "planning part of a school curriculum in relation to one or more school subjects" (Sabar, Rudduck, & Reid, 1987, p. 2). The mechanisms of teacher and school autonomy in the kibbutz have been changed, but many of them are still valid today and can contribute to curricular knowledge.

These seven principles can be discerned throughout this volume in the eight chapters, which make up three sections.

INTEGRATED CHILD AND YOUTH SERVICES
FOR CHILDREN AND ADULTS
FROM INSIDE AND OUTSIDE THE KIBBUTZ SOCIETY

1. Shafririm classes in Kibbutz Givat-Haim. Benjamin Shafrir and Abraham Herzog describe this unique special education institute that strengthens the "self" of each pupil according to the principles of kibbutz education.
2. Kfar Tikva is a younger institution (established in 1964) serving disabled adults. It has a central community that functions as a kibbutz while maintaining connections to the outer community in Tivon. Arie Pinkowitz, its manager, describes the past and present of this institution, which was established in the original buildings of kibbutz Givot Zeid.

CHILD AND YOUTH SERVICES
FOR DETACHED AND TROUBLED INDIVIDUALS
AND GROUPS FROM OUTSIDE THE KIBBUTZ

1. "The Project for the Education of Israeli Children in the Kibbutz Movement" was established in 1943 and is still active. This project aims at the absorption of individual children, including immigrants, in "foster families" of different kibbutzim. Edna Shoham and Neomi Shiloah describe an additional new model–the "foster family home" in the kibbutz–a married couple (or man and woman) that provide 10 children with a model of a functioning home.
2. Youth Aliyah groups ("Youth Societies") are the oldest vehicle of the kibbutz for both absorption of children from outside and for enlarging the children's and the kibbutz communities. Two other similar forms of absorption–the *moshavim* (a cooperative settlement less collective in organization than the kibbutz) and varied residential settings–were influenced by the model and principles of kibbutz education. Simha Shlasky summarizes and analyses the foundation of kibbutz identity through the historical process of the

"youth societies" of "Youth Aliyah." He details the kibbutz so-
cial-ideological point of view as well as the educational one.
3. "Social and Academic Integration of City and Kibbutz Youth," by
    Edna Shoham, is a comparison of two kibbutz secondary schools
    with other residential facilities. One is the Anne Frank Haven
    studied by Kohlberg and his successors, and the second is
    Gan-Shemuel, a program that was inspired by the Haven model.
    The two belong to the more leftist kibbutz movement, Kibbutz
    Artzi, where youth from the age of 13 live isolated from the kib-
    butz in the "educational *mosad* [institute]." Youth societies were
    absorbed in the old version of the *mosad* and in newer versions
    comprising many Russian immigrants.
4. The *Na'aleh* program (the Hebrew acronym for "youth immigrat-
    ing without or before their parents") is a unique way of absorbing
    young Russian immigrants in kibbutzim and other varied residen-
    tial settings. Orit Bendas-Jacob describes this new model of Youth
    Aliyah and compares the kibbutz schools to the non-kibbutz
    schools that share the same approach.

REGIONAL CHILD AND YOUTH SERVICES THAT INCLUDE KIBBUTZ AND NON-KIBBUTZ CHILDREN WHO CONTINUE LIVING AT HOME WHILE ATTENDING KIBBUTZ INSTITUTIONS

1. "Integration in Kibbutz Day Schools" illustrates an example of the
    regionalization of secondary and elementary kibbutz schools. Since
    1972, some daily schools of the Beit-Shean valley absorbed dis-
    abled pupils within the national policy of educational integration. I
    describe the historical story, added by an analysis of the process
    and the vehicles of integration.
2. "The Zweig Center for Special Education at Oranim" is based on a
    school-university partnership that follows the heritage of kibbutz
    special education. The center is located in the academic Kibbutz
    Teachers College at Oranim. Its methods of partnership with kib-
    butz and non-kibbutz special education pupils are rooted in the de-
    velopmental process of special education in the kibbutz movement
    from the 1940s.

In addition to the seven kibbutz education principles, the chapters of
this volume have some other common features:

1. "Community" is a basic term in all these cases: The inner communities of the child and youth services, the outer communities around the kibbutz (regional, national and international), the kibbutz "foster families," and the institutions in-between.
2. There is a "totality" dimension in all the services, even in the daily schools and college. The "unity of educational factors" from the kibbutz education heritage is rooted in all the examples of this special collection. The educational community is part of its social community. The totality works according to the historical example of the kibbutz.
3. There are varied educational "frameworks" (structures/institutions) covering many educational factors that assist and complement each other: Daily schools and residential settings; special education schools and tracks in regular schools; individual and group frameworks; formal and informal frameworks; local and regional organizations; elementary, secondary, and higher education.
4. The historical heritage of kibbutz (special) education is the foundation of all the services.
5. The services are based dually on kibbutz educational practices and on educational theory.
6. The services are analyzed using research methods that can be used as "analysis schemes" and for future planning. The methods are for the most part descriptive, historical, and qualitative. The titles and sub-titles of the eight chapters in this collection have many "checklists" of characteristics of schools, frameworks, and organizations that are used internationally for the analysis of services or for planning new services. The principles of child and youth frameworks of the kibbutz and their methods of analysis can be applied beyond the kibbutz and Israel for past, present, and future services.

Yuval Dror

REFERENCES

Dror, Y. (1995). The Anne Frank Haven in an Israeli kibbutz. *Adolescence, 30* (119), 617-629.

Kohlberg, L. (1985). The just community approach to moral education in theory and practice. In M. Berkowitz & F. Oser (Eds.), *Moral education* (27-87). Hillside, NJ: Erlbaum.

Sabar, N., Rudduck, J., & Reid, W. (Eds.). (1987). *Partnership and autonomy in school-based curriculum development: Policies and practices in Israel and England.* Sheffield: Division of Education, University of Sheffield.

Shafririm:
The Institute for Special Education

Benjamin Shafrir
Abraham Hertzog

SUMMARY. Shafririm–the Institute of Special Education–is situated within Kibbutz Givat Haim Ichud and was founded in 1957. Its purpose was to provide an alternative educational framework for pupils who had experienced difficulties within the mainstream kibbutz schools. The school now includes over 300 pupils between the ages of 12 to 21. It is the largest special education framework in Israel for this age group. Pupils come from all over Israel. Those whose homes are not within travelling distance live with foster families in settlements in the surrounding area. Among the special characteristics of the school is its integration in and use of kibbutz facilities, including the various work "branches" of the communal settlement: This as part of its educational, therapeutic, and rehabilitative philosophy. *[Article copies available for a fee from The Haworth Document Delivery Service: 1-800-342-9678. E-mail address: <getinfo@ haworthpressinc.com> Website: <http://www.HaworthPress.com> © 2001 by The Haworth Press, Inc. All rights reserved.]*

KEYWORDS. Kibbutz special education, community education, milieu therapy, foster care, inclusive education, community integration

---

Benjamin Shafrir and Abraham Hertzog are affiliated with Shafririm Institute at the Kibbutz Givat Haim Ichud.

[Haworth co-indexing entry note]: "Shafririm: The Institue for Special Education." Shafrir, Benjamin, and Abraham Hertzog. Co-published simultaneously in *Child & Youth Services* (The Haworth Press, Inc.) Vol. 22, No. 1/2, 2001, pp. 7-21; and: *Innovative Approaches in Working with Children and Youth: New Lessons from the Kibbutz* (ed: Yuval Dror) The Haworth Press, Inc., 2001, pp. 7-21. Single or multiple copies of this article are available for a fee from The Haworth Document Delivery Service [1-800-342-9678, 9:00 a.m. - 5:00 p.m. (EST). E-mail address: getinfo@haworthpressinc.com].

7

The opposing ideologies of integration or segregation of special education and regular education services are known to everyone in the field of education. This controversy has also reached the educators of the kibbutzim, and two opposite approaches are present in kibbutz schools. One group of kibbutzim invested large amounts of economic resources, manpower, and creative thinking in order not to separate those in need of special education from other children in their age group. Other kibbutzim invested in finding optimal conditions for those with special education needs in separate schools in the nearby surroundings that could satisfy their needs. These children returned home every afternoon to their natural environment. Children from locations where there were no such facilities were sent to such schools during the week but returned home for weekends. Shafririm is an example of such a program. Children and youth from this school are placed with foster families in the school's vicinity.

During the last 40 to 50 years, kibbutzim made compromises between segregation and integration approaches. The dichotomous choice was replaced by a choice between learning centers, workshops, and integrated classrooms. Most of these programs were created in regional schools, and the rationale for sending a child to such a setting was based on his or her cognitive ability. The main criteria were–and are to this day–the ability to take part in lessons, master basic skills (reading, writing, and arithmetic), and abstraction: learning abilities. Child guidance clinics assisted schools by diagnosing children according to neurological function and suggesting ways of treating disabilities, especially dyslexia, dyscalculia, lack of sensory-motor integration, and so forth.

In integrative education, there was an interesting development 30 years ago concerning children's caretakers, specifically, the *mememiot,* the special caretakers who attended to the children's needs. In the beginning they were expected to function as the "listening ear" and the warm hand that both directs and nurtures the child with special needs. However, as integrative education advanced, the definition of *mememiot* slowly changed, first to *mekasheret* (contact person), then to teacher's helper and, among the more ambitious, many went on to study counseling.

It seemed that this progress affected only the educators, while children who were first regarded as young persons in personal distress were now regarded as angry, hurt, and rebellious under-achievers. Their diagnosis was now often evaluated "efficiently" in numbers and abbreviations; thus his or her true personality was misinterpreted. We invest so much in "innovative changes" we forget that education is a process that fosters changes through advancing the individual, enriching his experiences, and regaining his self-integrity: the true meaning of rehabilitation. The Shafririm Special Education School chose these latter standards as the basis for its educational work.

BACKGROUND INFORMATION

The Shafririm Institute of Special Education was founded in 1957 by Benjamin Shafrir. Its purpose was to provide a supportive framework for pupils from Kibbutz Givat Haim and from the neighboring settlements that were in need of special education. Prior to the establishment of Shafririm, special education pupils from the kibbutz were placed in schools that were usually located in towns. The purpose of establishing the Institute within the kibbutz was to provide a local solution for the needs of these pupils without severing the connection with their peer group and their lives on the kibbutz.

Shafrir established a day school providing an educational, therapeutic, and rehabilitative environment for pupils with varied educational and related behavioral problems. For the first few years there were no selection criteria based on learning and behavioral disabilities. However, the common denominators of these pupils were learning difficulties together with the accompanying sense of personal failure and an inability to integrate with other students and the social framework of their kibbutz peer group.

Considerable experience accumulated and a good reputation achieved for finding creative solutions for pupils with learning and behavioral difficulties. For these reasons the kibbutz movement encouraged the Institute to expand activities in two directions. One was to enlarge the Institute by accepting pupils from kibbutzim all over Israel and not only the immediate area. The second was to act as advisors and facilitators in the creation and development of similar programs in other kibbutzim. This included programs in Degania Alef, Shaar HaNegev, Ramat David, Kfar Blum, Yavneh, and Sulam Tzor.

At Givat Haim we began accepting pupils from other kibbutzim for whom there was a clear indication of the necessity of removing them from their kibbutz homes. However, special emphasis was laid on strengthening long-term connection to their natural, educational, and social environment. These pupils lived with foster families in settlements in the surrounding area (but not on the kibbutz) for 5 days a week and then returned to their kibbutzim on the weekends and holidays and for any special activities in which their peer group was involved. As a result of our success, the Ministry of Education and local or urban educational authorities began sending pupils who could not adapt to the demands of the regular school system.

Today–40 years later–the Institute has a student population of 303: one hundred thirteen pupils of middle school age and 190 high school pupils. Fifty-eight pupils live with foster families (Sunday through Thursday). Two-hundred forty-five are brought by bus to and from home every day. The pupils come from 117 different settlements throughout Israel: eighty-two of them from 46 different kibbutzim and the rest from non-kibbutz villages and large cities. The decrease in proportion of students from kibbutzim reflects the considerable changes that have occurred within the kibbutz educational system over the past generation. From a starting point of inflexible academic streaming, the majority of kibbutz schools now provide a much more comprehensive and flexible educational service for their pupils. The result is that the majority of pupils with learning disabilities can now continue their education at their kibbutz school, and only in those cases where the kibbutz school is not capable of providing a solution for the particular needs of the student will he or she be referred to Shafririm.

THE PUPILS

In 40 years close to 1,900 pupils of both sexes have graduated from the Institute. The vast majority are rehabilitated model citizens who have served in the army, work for their living, are married, and are parents to functioning children.

The phrase "special education" is an over-generalized term that does not adequately define the subject and in particular the object: the pupil. The combination of the words "special" and "education" results in negative associations relating to "exceptional students." For this reason we do not think in the negative terms of "the exceptional student" but instead we see our students as being "different." This difference challenges us to provide a special educational environment whose methods and aims are to deal with those different and special needs of each pupil. Thus our methods include a study program tailored to the individual needs and abilities of each pupil. We take into account the pace at which pupils absorb and master learning skills. We constantly assess and encourage them in developing their abilities and potential not only as "learning students" but also as human beings. From the above it will be clear that we are involved with 303 separate and special "universes."

Nevertheless, we can point to a number of problems that are common to most of our students. We can describe the essence of these problems in the word "distress." Each and every one of our pupils, at his or her own particular level of self-comprehension and self-awareness, directly or indirectly expresses his or her "distress" at the situation. He or she feels a failure because of rejection by the regular school. We try to be constantly aware of these feelings of failure and rejection which are part of our pupils' psychic baggage.

An additional characteristic, in direct reaction to feelings of failure and rejection, is that they suffer from low self-esteem accompanied by feelings of inferiority and anger. They search for ways to justify these feelings of being victims of discrimination and failures.

Since the assessment of pupils is complex and is based on psychological and, if necessary, neurological tests, it is appropriate to describe the pupils of our Institute in accordance with the etiological difficulties from which they suffer.

Nineteen percent suffer from "minimal retardation." This requires a study program that places special emphasis on their difficulties with abstraction, generalization, and conceptualization. Twenty-five percent of our students suffer from varied emotional difficulties. These pupils have average IQ levels. Their difficulties are expressed through low self-esteem; extreme variations in mood; a lack of motivation, self-discipline, or self-control; and extreme acting out. Together with the lack of interpersonal communication skills, all of these are accompanied by a low frustration level.

Fifty-six percent of our pupils suffer from learning disabilities resulting from neuropsychological deficiencies. Clearly this is the most heterogeneous group in every way. It includes those with low attention span as well as hyperactive pupils (ADHD). This group includes slow learners who are hypo-kinetic as well as pupils who suffer from organic disabilities such as cerebral palsy and epilepsy.

The heterogeneity within this group also finds expression in the wide variation of measured intelligence, from dyslexic pupils with an IQ of 130 to students with an IQ of 90 but a potential for higher achievement, given the right form of intervention. We should emphasize that dyslexic pupils are referred to us not because of their "technical learning problems" but because of the frustrations they have suffered in the regular school where they were treated as slow learners suffering from difficulties in basic comprehension.

THE STAFF

Presently our staff has 89 members: thirty-three are members of Kibbutz Givat Haim Ichud and 56 are salaried workers from outside the kibbutz. An important and unusual factor to be noted is the relatively large number of male staff members–29. Seventy-seven are teachers, 5 are counselors (a psychologist and social workers), 7 are administrative workers, a headmistress, and an educational consultant. Regardless of the specific role of each staff member, everybody–without exception–has personal contact with the students.

For the kibbutz, the Institute is one of the most important "branches" that over the years has provided employment for large numbers of members. Often they start work in ancillary roles without formal training or experience, and only after proving that they are suitable for at least a period of two years are they sent to study in order to obtain the necessary academic qualifications. Those individual members of staff are "absorbed" and educated in a way very similar to new students. This "organic" form of absorption contributes to the family atmosphere among staff members (Shafrir, 1985).

In contrast to most educational units, our staff members do not suffer from "burn out." Our staff is stable and each of us continues year in and year out. Needless to say, at the end of the year we are tired and exhausted, but at the beginning of the next academic year we return with refueled emotional and educational batteries, as it is written in the Israeli pioneer's song, *Lakum machar baboker, im shir hadash balev* (to wake up in the morning with a new song in our hearts).

The individual and collective strength of our staff showed itself four years ago on the retirement of Benjamin Shafrir, the founder and only principal for 36 years. His place was filled by Noa Levy, a kibbutz member who has worked in the Institute for many years. The "changing of the guard" took place without difficulty because of the dedication and self-confidence of staff members.

It is important to point out that despite the professional quality and dedication of staff members, this educational venture would not have lasted without the acceptance and support of the kibbutz community which perceives the Institute as an "economic branch" with moral values that deserve their support.

THE PROGRAM OF THE INSTITUTE

In contrast to the generally accepted practice in Israeli special education, our students are not placed in classes in accordance with their diag-
nosed difficulties. Thus one finds virtually all the possible learning
disabilities in pupils of the same class. Age is not a primary factor in
placement, so that within the one class there can be a 3 to 4 year age
span between pupils. Similarly, learning capacity and achievement is
not a decisive factor. What is decisive is the social compatibility of the
pupil: his social needs and his ability to give and receive social rein-
forcements. From the above it follows that every year we totally re-or-
ganize each pupil's classroom placement according to the social skills
that he has developed in the preceding year. In this matching process we
take into account one of the most important factors of all: the personality of the classroom educator. From the above the reader will understand that we fulfil the principles of a multi-layered "home" for special
education.

Shafririm teaches formal educational and academic skills even though
these are not goals in themselves but merely a means for achieving our
educational goals: to bring about changes in each pupil, to encourage
self-growth and individual development, to widen horizons and strengthening their ability to adapt and survive, but above all to raise the pupil's
feeling of self-esteem and self-confidence.

We emphasize vocational education as a means of achieving technical skills and also to emphasize "work" as a primary value in itself. We
encourage art and craft activities in order to help students develop skills
in self-expression for themselves and to the outside world.

THE INSTITUTE AND THE KIBBUTZ COMMUNITY

A first-time visitor to Shafririm can, on arrival, mistakenly go to
Misgav, the neighboring elementary school. There are no external differences between the two institutions. They use common facilities such
as the kibbutz swimming pool, sports facilities, and the communal dining room. At these places we develop the integration between our autonomous educational institute and the kibbutz community.

The school is situated within the kibbutz and is an integral part of the
human environment and the kibbutz community. Pupils eat breakfast
and lunch in the communal dining room together with the kibbutz members. Apart from the basic function of providing good quality food, the

meals are an important part of the pupil's daily schedule. We use them to develop our wider educational aims of integrating our pupils by presenting them with situations in which they have to behave in a normative manner. This special situation in the communal dining room allows us to understand their difficulties and limitations and their behavioral patterns. These give us clearer indications as to what points need to be dealt with more specifically and on a deeper level. Other facilities belonging to the kibbutz and available to the school are the squash court, the educational zoo, the riding stables, and, when necessary, we have recourse to other educational, agricultural, and service branches of the kibbutz which we use to assist us in our integrative educational process.

FOSTER FAMILIES:
EDUCATIONAL AND THERAPEUTIC PRINCIPLES

The foster family experience is an important element of pupil growth because:

1. Fostering enables integration into another family to learn how to cope with behaviors different from those that they typically use.
2. Fostering enables pupils to develop new and sometimes intimate relationships in an unfamiliar environment. These relationships are not "therapeutic," so that this experience of the pupil in a new environment presents him with the challenge of contending with a different reality. Clearly this takes place in a protected environment but without any distortion of this different reality. The pupils develop self-confidence in their new environment and learn what their strengths and weaknesses are in adapting to the conditions of a given environment.
3. Fostering enables pupils to gain experience in areas that are not available to their peers, particularly those from kibbutzim. These include the independent use of public transport, the use of money and knowledge of prices, and contact with unfamiliar people and life patterns.
4. Fostering exposes the pupil to many different facets of life, and depending on the skill and effectiveness of our directed intervention, there will be a commensurate positive development of character. This makes a significant contribution to our program of "directed differentiation."
5. Fostering leads to the possibility of "transference" of problematic, even traumatic situations, and the social workers encourage the

development of situations of counter-transference. Thus the events that take place in the foster family include possibilities for sublimation and a field for experimentation in gaining positive therapeutic experiences. Clearly there is a danger that the opposite can happen with a family so that the process can become pathogenic. In such a situation, we find an alternative, suitable foster family for the pupil and use the change as part of the therapeutic process.

6. The experience of fostering provides a variety of opportunities for relating to the specific needs of each individual pupil with particular emphasis on the development of inter-personal relationships.

The placement and matching of pupils within foster families is a complex and sensitive process. It requires knowledge, experience, and intuition on the part of the social workers. They have to take into account the "chemistry" and the dynamics of the interpersonal relationships that exist between all those involved in the process: (a) The pupil and the foster family, (b) the pupil and the environment of the foster family, (c) other children who live with and share a room with our pupil, and (d) the family of origin and the foster family.

Only children above the age of 13 or 14 are placed in foster families, because the needs of younger pupils are so great that the average foster family is unable to fulfil them. It is important to emphasize that before kibbutz schools became more comprehensive and flexible, the majority of our students needed to be placed in foster families. Today this is the case with only 20% of our pupils.

We are often asked, "Why not an internal boarding school within the grounds of the kibbutz?" Our answer to this question is an unequivocal "No." A boarding school within the kibbutz would increase the alienation of our pupils and their feelings of not belonging. These feelings of being different and suffering from discrimination would only increase their sense of failure. This is in direct contradiction to our stated aims of deepening and strengthening the connection with their environment.

However, we do not want to deny the benefits that can be achieved by partly removing a pupil from his natural environment. Taking all the above into account, a basic condition for accepting a pupil to Shafririm is the absence of over-riding reasons for removing him totally from his natural environment.

Over the years we have learned that the effective combination for our pupils is a study day that ends after lunch, spending time with the foster family in the afternoon and evening, combined with a return to their family of origin for Thursday afternoon through Saturday. This combination builds a rehabilitative framework suited to the needs of our pupils.

THE EDUCATIONAL AIMS OF THE INSTITUTE

The effective treatment of children with learning and behavioral disabilities depends to a large extent on the proper diagnostic identification of the basic reasons for their damaged functioning. This process enables us to identify at an early stage the developmental path of each child and the etiology that lies at the root of his flawed behaviors. We can then adjust his study program with the aim of maximizing his personal development and rehabilitation. Before we describe the stated goals of the school it is important to point out the major behavioral and performance characteristics of our pupils (Shafrir, 1985). These include:

- *Behavioral disorders* of hyperactivity that are sometimes a symptom but principally is undirected and unfocussed activity. Often these behaviors are identified by sudden and unexpected changes in pupils' behavioral patterns.
- *Short attention span* in motor activity but principally in comprehension and thinking. These are difficulties in keeping up with continuing activities over a period of time.
- *Emotional instability* characterized by ups and downs and mood changes.
- *Lack of social skills.*
- *Poor work and study habits* shown by a lack of systematic thinking and performance characterized by uneven thinking processes.
- *Impulsiveness* and a lack of psychomotor stability.
- *Specific learning disorders* in reading, writing, spelling, and mathematical comprehension. There may also be difficulties in abstraction, generalization, conceptualization, and integration.

These provide a hint of the diagnostic difficulties in differentiation between children with neurological impairments and those suffering from dysfunctional behaviors as a result of emotional problems. It is necessary to emphasize that:

1. Behavioral disturbance in a child suffering from inadequate performance is only partially a result of neurological disorder. These behaviors are *not* permanent and unchangeable.

2. Dysfunctional behaviors are to a substantial extent an integral part of the relationship between the child and his environment.
3. Inadequate, inappropriate, and incomprehensible behaviors contribute to the unstable relationship between the child and his natural environment.
4. Complications and misunderstandings between the child and his environment can be rectified and improved by educational and social therapy and appropriate rehabilitation.

Thus we see that pupils who attend Shafririm have additional common characteristics apart from their difficulties in learning and adaptation. These are a negative self-image, failure in learning and adaptation to the environment, absence of ability to comprehend and absorb learning material, and social situations with a paucity of positive experiences.

When we first meet with the pupil, his parents, and his educators we emphasize that our primary goal is to bring about changes in his self-image. Even though our pupils attend an institution whose goals are study and education oriented, they soon learn that learning is not in itself a goal but only a means to provide positive experiences and moments of success and creativity.

Another important aim is to take all possible measures so that the pupil will continue to be an integral member of his peer group. The realization of this goal is problematic in non-kibbutz environments. Nevertheless, we make efforts to integrate pupils in social activities such as youth and sport groups in their home environment.

The third important aim is to ensure the pupil's acceptance and belonging to a peer group and over a period of time exchanging the dependence that is created by a healthy relationship.

As already mentioned, the pupil attends a school whose goals are vocational and craft-centered, in which teaching is a process of educational rehabilitation, so that from the first moments in school the pupil studies according to a program that requires initiative and flexibility but within a structured framework. From the outset it is made clear that there are different expectations of every pupil in terms of study, behavioral patterns, and over-all progress towards change. Each pupil is valued according to his own ability and related to his specific needs with a special emphasis on functional, social relationships.

The result of the pupil's exposure to this atmosphere shows itself within 6-12 months after arrival. At the beginning of the second year he or she becomes an "active agent" in helping to absorb new pupils. Staff members and his peer group make extra efforts to help them. For the second year pupil, this is perhaps the first real experience of "altruistic giving." The result of this exposure to the vocational and crafts curriculum is expressed through the strengthening of "self" through achieving "status" accompanied by a personal need to fill this changing self-image with content. Changes in the self-image of the pupil become evident in the home environment so that his parents become active partners in encouraging him to gain technical proficiency. Here an important factor is the attitude of the kibbutz work manager in providing opportunities to attain this technical proficiency.

Our educational program is not based on a "system" of techniques, inflexible principles, and routine or fixed perceptions. Thus instead of talking in terms of a "specified working system," we think of "different and varied working styles" through which each of our staff members expresses his personality, his working principles, and his overall world view. In other words we are describing a collection of different styles, the combination of which produce the ethos of the school and its overall atmosphere. This is similar to an orchestra in which different instruments produce different notes but work in harmony to produce the resulting melody. We should remember also that the pupils too are part of this "harmonic" orchestra.

CONCLUSION

The basis of our work is educational, social, and therapeutic rehabilitation in which we aim to expose pupils and staff to learning and therapeutic experiences of deep significance.

The pupils arrive at the Institute suffering from damaged self-esteem, poor self-image, and a lack of confidence in themselves. These are accompanied by feelings of under-achievement in all aspects of their lives within the educational system. It is obvious that in such an extreme situation our main initial efforts are designed to provide a series of "successes," but we do so without covering up the pupils' limitations. We emphasize that "to be different" is not necessarily "to be exceptional." The proverb, "Educate the child according to the way he chooses," forms the basis of our educational philosophy and working methods. The pupil as an individual is at the center. We make every effort to adapt ourselves to his specific needs, constantly taking into consideration each individual's talents and abilities.

Our primary goal is to promote changes in our pupils (Shafrir, 1985). The pupils are actively involved in planning their program of study. Great efforts are made to match the program to the overall needs and desires of the pupils, but despite our orientation towards satisfying the needs of each individual pupil, we place special emphasis on encouraging and strengthening the process of socialization and on the acceptance of values and norms of co-operation, mutual help, and social activity. All these have the aim of developing social skills that will benefit pupils when they are inducted into the army or join the world of working adults.

At the beginning of each year pupils plan their individual study schedule on the basis of their personal preferences and the various possibilities that are open to them. Through this process they become active partners in choosing the fields of interest. They become responsible for their own decisions. The task of the class educators is to assist, direct, and encourage the further development of the pupil's responsibility and initiative. In addition, they remain open to the pupil's suggestions for changes in the study schedule during the course of the school year.

Thus the essential atmosphere of the institute is that of "a home for education." Our method is through studying and lessons. Amongst our pupils are those who will deal with national matriculation examinations as well as those whose aims are to gain the basic learning skills. But in our relationships with the pupils we emphasize and remind ourselves that study is a means and not an end in itself, and as a means it has value only if it promotes changes.

At the school we operate a considerable number of study centers where one can find pupils from different classes at the same time. Of course there are lessons attended by the whole class, but most of the studying takes place in groups and sub-groups. In this way there is the greatest possibility of providing the individual attention that each pupil needs in order to encourage development in accordance with his or her level, abilities, gifts and individual rhythm.

Shafririm places the "self" of the child as the central focus of its efforts and operates in accordance with the "10 Commandments" set out below (Shafrir, 1985):

1. Synchronization between the pupil's daily timetable, his pace of life, and the experiences of his home environment.
2. Attractive and interesting fields of learning.

3. Learning as a means and not an end in itself.
4. Emphasis on creativity and vocational ability to achieve relief from frustration and to guide the pupils away from impulsiveness and toward creative and positive actions.
5. Emphasis on the value of the individual: "From each according to his ability to each according to his needs."
6. A value system different from the generally accepted values of over-achievement and an emphasis on avoiding frustrating competitive situations.
7. Encouragement of personal growth and acceptance of responsibility.
8. Belief in the undiscovered abilities that are hidden in each and every individual pupil.
9. Practical and realistic orientation towards the pupil's problems without covering up their limitations in adapting to society.
10. Realization of the positive qualities of each and every pupil and their utilization in the pupil's integration into the wider society.

From a small framework founded in 1957 for 12 pupils from the kibbutz, Shafririm has become a comprehensive and unique institution. The contribution of the school to individual personal rehabilitation is best expressed in the words of a graduating pupil: "When I came to Shafririm I was 'something.' I now leave as 'someone.'"

AUTHOR NOTES

Benjamin Shafrir was (1950-1957) the co-director of the Tokayer Residential Treatment Home for children. In 1957 he founded and headed the Institute for special education at kibbutz Givat Haim Ichud (later–"Shafririm" School). He served as representative of the World Zionist Organization in Scandinavia (1975-1978) and from the mid 60s to the mid 80s was the senior consultant to the Child and Family Clinic of the Ichud (and later Taka) kibbutz movements.

Abraham Hertzog is working in "Shafririm" as educator (and later co-director) from 1962 onwards. He served as representative of the Department of Education (Jewish Agency) in Cape-town (South Africa) (1967-1970), as a supervisor of counselors in the Ministry of Education (1973-1975) and from the mid 70s as a consultant for special education in the kibbutz movement's regional clinics.

REFERENCE

Shafrir, B. (1985). *To be involved.* Tel-Aviv: Hakibbutz Hameuchad. (in Hebrew).

APPENDIX
TECHNICAL AND VOCATIONAL EDUCATION

Cooking
Sewing
Office management
Motor vehicle maintenance
Motor vehicle electricity
Metalwork
Carpentry
Plastics
Technological exposure
House maintenance
Design and production of learning aids
Computers
Plant nursery and gardening
Animal care
Industrial rehabilitation unit connected to Keter Plastic (an industrial company)

EDUCATIONAL AND THERAPEUTIC SERVICES
LEARNING CENTERS

Sport
Music
Nature
Computers
Mathematics
English
Communication
Art (drawing, sculpture, arts and crafts)
Tractor driving
Automobile driving
Education and preparation for work
Seamanship (including sailing abroad to Greece or Turkey)
Lifesaving course
Library and study center
Survival course
Games center
Rhythmotherapy
Diagnosis of learning and behavioral problems
Crisis intervention
Psychiatric supervision
Therapeutic horse riding
Dance therapy
Music therapy
Animal therapy
Reflexology
Community involvement project
Preparation for induction into the army
Physical therapy using "Alexander" system
Rehabilitative swimming
Speech therapy
Group dynamics
Sex and family education
Dining etiquette

Kfar Tikva–Therapeutic Concept for People with Special Needs: Knock, Knock, Knock . . . Is Someone Out There?

Arie Pencovici

SUMMARY. Kfar Tikva, for persons with special needs, has evolved from an institution-like setting into a kibbutz-like community and now is working to achieve full-citizenship status for residents and non-residents alike. Common principles of services for people with disabilities such as deinstitutionalization, normalization, inclusion, least restrictive environment, and mainstreaming worked well in the past, but they have become obstacles to complete decision-making authority and self-determination. Kfar-Tikva is committed to (a) help residents make choices regarding their personal and social life, (b) provide "tools" for effective choice and decision-making including social, educational, and vocational tools, and (c) become an economically and legally independent community based on kibbutz principles or those of any freely-chosen community. *[Article copies available for a fee from The Haworth Document Delivery Service: 1-800-342-9678. E-mail address: <getinfo@haworthpressinc.com> Website: <http://www.HaworthPress. com> © 2001 by The Haworth Press, Inc. All rights reserved.]*

KEYWORDS. Special needs, community education, human rights, community integration, human services, developmental disabilities

---

Arie Pencovici is affiliated with Kfar Tikva.

[Haworth co-indexing entry note]: "Kfar Tikva–Therapeutic Concept for People with Special Needs: Knock, Knock, Knock . . . Is Someone Out There?" Pencovici, Arie. Co-published simultaneously in *Child & Youth Services* (The Haworth Press, Inc.) Vol. 22, No. 1/2, 2001, pp. 23-36; and: *Innovative Approaches in Working with Children and Youth: New Lessons from the Kibbutz* (ed: Yuval Dror) The Haworth Press, Inc., 2001, pp. 23-36. Single or multiple copies of this article are available for a fee from The Haworth Document Delivery Service [1-800-342-9678, 9:00 a.m. - 5:00 p.m. (EST). E-mail address: getinfo@haworthpressinc.com].

Kfar Tikva has evolved over the last 30 years from an institution-like setting of adult people with special needs into a kibbutz-like community and, lately, into a program where more than 70 of 200 participants live in the neighboring community surrounding it. Today most of the new residents entering the program come with the intention of continuing to live in communities outside of Kfar Tikva (with our support).

In the residential community, residents participate actively with management and staff in all decision-making and planning processes. For example, they are represented on the residents' committee, the social and cultural activities committee, and so forth. In this fashion, cooperation between residents, staff, and management is continually enacted. Also, the organizational set-up is based on that of a true community. Residents live in separate houses for one or two residents instead of in dormitories. The communal buildings (for example, the dining room and community center) are centrally located. As in a kibbutz, residents are free to choose at any given time between the advantages offered by communal living or the privacy of their own homes.

Is Kfar Tikva a typical example? Democracy is a well-established policy in most modern societies and countries. The basic human rights of people are universally accepted and recognized . . . in principle. Despite all this, in some of the so-called modern countries you can still find places where people with special needs are segregated, confined, and put away from the eyes of society and treated as objects as though everything that has to do with human rights does not include them. Some of those institutions even call themselves "friends of humanity."

Other institutions, who call themselves "green villages" or "organic villages," deny people with special needs their basic human rights by forcing them to eat specific foods or behave in specific ways which, de facto, means denying them the basic right to decide for themselves. For instance, watching TV is forbidden because it presents a lot of violence, and eating at McDonald's is forbidden because it pollutes the body with toxic food. We believe that adopting these credos for oneself is perfectly legitimate but forcing someone else to behave according to the beliefs of the institution's management is, in our opinion, a basic and unlawful denial of human rights. That includes the right to have sex whenever they feel like it and without the interference or approval of anyone beside themselves.

We must remind the reader that people with special needs have not committed any crime and are not confined to institutions, hostels, or group homes because their behavior is detrimental to society. But the simple fact that they are under the care of "so-called professionals" exposes them to the personal or institutional beliefs of staff and management.

Two hundred fifty years ago the French Revolution opened a huge "gate" over which we find the inscription "liberte, egalite, fraternite." Gates such as this one spread all over the world and millions passed under them, changing their lives, providing them with dignity and self-respect. Can people with special needs also pass under these gates? Are these gates for them also? Based on the same philosophy, many other gates or doors were erected with "normalization," "inclusion," "least restrictive environment," and "mainstreaming" inscribed on them. These are beautiful doors with promising labels.

You knock at the door: "Is anyone at home?" You try to open it. It is open but then you discover that there is nobody and nothing behind the door–no house, no building, no people–just a door standing in the middle of nothing with a sparkling label appearing on both sides so that from whichever direction you come you get to the same place: nowhere. You are in the desert of human understanding.

How can it be that after all those democratic and human rights labels we still see institutions or pseudo-communities being built just under the nose of or, even worse, with the help of so-called advanced professional decision-makers? How is it not yet clear that people with special needs must live only in the community with their basic human rights safe-guarded as for any other human being? Maybe we are knocking at the wrong doors. Maybe we should try knocking at integrity's door or maybe at politicians' doors. We are sure that someone is there but we are not so sure they will open the door.

The title of this article is "Kfar Tikva: Therapeutic Concept for People with Special Needs." I carefully chose the word "concept" and not community or village. We prefer to speak of a concept and not of a geographical location. A concept transcends a specific place. It can be implemented anywhere but Kfar Tikva is located in northern Israel and began as a kibbutz-like community for people with special needs. It is imperative that we state from the beginning that if we were to begin a new service for people with special needs today, we would never create a segregated community in which people with special needs live outside a normal community.

These beliefs come from our experience at Kfar Tikva, and I begin with a description of Kfar Tikva's past and present. Then two aspects of Kfar Tikva as part of the wider community will be described: the quality of service and academic studies.

THE THERAPEUTIC CONCEPT
OF KFAR TIKVA

In the last decade, with the appearance of such concepts as normalization and de-institutionalization, we have witnessed a growing trend towards the transfer of people with special needs from institutions to the community.

Institutions are perceived as "self-contained social systems that allow house staff and various practitioners to exercise a substantial measure of social control with little outside influence" (De Jong, 1978). The effects of prolonged institutionalization are considered dehumanizing and harmful.

> Patients are encouraged to follow instructions, rules and regulations. Compliance is highly valued, and individualistic behavior is discouraged. The "good" patient is the individual who respectfully follows instructions and does not disagree with the staff. On the other hand the patient who constantly asks for a dime for the pay phone, a postage stamp, or a pass to leave the institution on personal business, tends to be treated as a nuisance or labeled "manipulative." Patients do not make their own appointments, keep their own medical charts, or take their own medication. Responsibility for these things is legally vested in the institution. (Corcoran, 1978)

W. Wolfensberger (1979) concluded that "People and society 'need' devaluated people and groups. This suggests that deviance-making and labeling are something inherent in human social functioning."

Institutions, which are seen as "inhuman," "big," and "bad" according to these views must be closed and residents transferred to hostels, group homes, and supervised staff apartments, which are "human," "small," and "good." We are living in a modern, dynamic and changing society where labels change with the same dynamism. This is one of the principles of normalization. However, it was previously noted that labeling is part of our nature. De-institutionalization helps to overcome this paradox. Not only do we transfer residents from institutions to the community, but we also transfer the label from people with special needs to the institutions: "All institutions are bad." This expression permits us to continue being "natural labelers" and also humanitarians. We stop labeling people and we begin labeling institutions. Hostels, group homes, and supervised staff apartments are also small institutions like the family. Is it a scientific fact that institutions are dehumanized, robot-run systems? Is it a scientific fact that the goals and rights of people with special needs can't be met in institutions?

The "Community Imperative" has become a credo. The transfer of people from institutions to the community has achieved national and international proportions. Is our job "done" when the person with special needs is relocated in the community? The "wave" of de-institutionalization is "washing" hundreds of people out of institutions into the community, many of them still living under continuous staff control, alienated and ignored, if not worse, by neighbors.

Normalization defined by W. Wolfensberger means: "Utilization of means which are as culturally normative as possible in order to establish and/or maintain personal behavior and characteristics which are as culturally normative as possible." There is no reference in this definition to the wishes or permission of people with special needs to be "normalized." Some of the candidates for normalization are considered to be at a level too low for them to express their opinion on the matter. But the wave washes all. Normalization is "good," so why wouldn't they want it?

We are not in favor of a principle that wants to "help" or force the person with special needs to act as normally or as normatively as possible. This gives a free hand to the imagination of professionals and researchers how to develop new techniques for transforming people who are different into people who *act* like us. It is assumed that we normal, intelligent people know what is better for others, especially for those who are "idiots," "imbeciles," or who have a "mental age of 6" and are commonly called mentally retarded.

We must not focus on transforming people into copies of ourselves, but help them decide what they want to be and how they want to act. It should not be our goal to induce or help people conform culturally and socially, although sometimes it seems we are doing this either consciously or unconsciously. I would posit as a goal the attempt to help the person who is labeled a person with special needs to make his own decisions about life. To help in making these decisions we should supply him with educational, social, and vocational "tools." The offer of these "tools" must be made through a process which enhances self-respect, self-confidence, social identification, capacity for criticism, and assertiveness.

It is my belief that the person with special needs should be helped to reduce his special needs to a minimum and not just act, dress, and live like a normal person. We should not forget that what strongly differentiates between a so-called normal person and a person with special needs is the capacity of the former to decide, based on previous knowledge, experience, and intuition. Transferring people from one place to another is not training to use intuition or teaching how to use previous knowledge and experience. Normal people decide for themselves where they want to live, how, and with whom. Anybody has the right to conform or be different. This is the privilege of decision-making, one of the highest of human rights, a right that should and must be shared by all. If some people have difficulty in exercising that right, it is our obligation to use all our professional and economic resources to help them but never to take over their privilege of decision-making. Kfar Tikva is an attempt to put these ideas into practice.

KFAR TIKVA IN PRACTICE:
PAST AND PRESENT

Kfar Tikva was founded 30 years ago as an institution for people with special needs. The aim was to establish a permanent work place and home for people with an I.Q. of between 45 and 75, assuring parents that their children would be cared for all their lives. Since the early 1970s, Kfar Tikva has been continually changing into a community modeled on the lines of the Israeli kibbutz.

The goals of the present-day Kfar Tikva community are: (a) to help residents make choices regarding their personal and social life, (b) to provide "tools" for effective choice and decision-making including social, educational, and vocational tools, and (c) to become an economically and legally independent community based on kibbutz principles or those of any freely-chosen community.

Kfar Tikva is situated between the Zebulun and Jezreel valleys on a 95-acre site near the town of Tivon. Formerly an abandoned kibbutz, Kfar Tikva consists of 100 houses, a modern kibbutz-like dining hall, and a community center containing a club, a music auditorium, and recreation rooms. The village has an indoor and outdoor sports facility, workshops, laundry, clinic, a swimming pool, a library, a plastics factory, and an alternative medicine center.

Presently the staff consists of the director, social workers, nurses, doctors, physical therapist, teachers and instructors. Sixty percent of the residents work as staff or semi-staff in the kitchen, garden, offices, clinic, laundry and house maintenance. The rest work in the workshops and factory. Many are employed outside the village in industry.

   The differences outlined below between the Kfar Tikva of yesterday and today exemplify the change in direction that has taken place in recent years. These differences can also be seen as indications of the major differences between what is known as life in a "traditional" institution and life in a community based on the kibbutz model.

In the past: Houses with 4 rooms, 4 people per room, and 2 bathrooms for 16 people. No privacy at all.

Today: Kibbutz-like apartments with 2 people in a 3-roomed apartment including a living-room, kitchen, and bathroom.

In the past: Permission and a pass were necessary for leaving the village, permission sometimes being denied as punishment for misbehavior.

Today: Residents are free to leave the village whenever they choose. The only punishment is expulsion from the village and this only in cases of serious and continuous deviant behavior.

In the past: The staff prepared and presided over the residents' daily schedule with specific times designated for work and sleep and compulsory attendance at meals.

Today: Residents are responsible for their own schedule. Only work is obligatory as a condition of residence. Residents can go to bed when they want. Although the dining-hall serves three meals a day, residents can prepare meals in their apartments if they wish.

In the past: The staff chose all educational, social, and recreational programs, including selecting films and the itineraries of all outings.

Today: Residents annually elect a cultural committee of 7-8 residents that makes these choices.

In the past: The staff decided which applicants for the program were accepted.

Today: Residents annually elect a New Residents' Committee of 7 residents that sends a 3 person delegation who, together with the social worker, doctor, and director, participate from the beginning in the process of acceptance or rejection of candidates. Sometimes a candidate has been accepted against the judgment of the staff, and the integration of that candidate has been successful, contrary to staff predictions.

In the past: The staff decided where residents worked.

Today: Residents decide. As in a kibbutz, kitchen, agricultural, and some maintenance tasks are shared by all residents. Every week a different group prepares breakfast and dinner. Residents draw up the list of names for this duty.

In the past: Residents spent their leisure time in the segregated village.

Today: In addition to voluntary activities arranged in the village, residents are encouraged to go to the nearest town for movies, folk dancing, theater and other cultural and social activities, or just for fun.

In the past: The staff made all decisions concerning the everyday life of the residents.

Today: Residents make decisions concerning their own lives such as what to eat, how to furnish their apartments, what to wear, what to plant in their private gardens and in the public gardens, where public phones should be situated, and so forth. These decisions are made by the elected Residents' Committee or by every individual resident.

In the past: Staff members hired new staff.

Today: Interviewing and hiring is conducted by a representative of the Residents' Committee together with the management.

In the past: Homosexual and heterosexual relations were forbidden.

Today: Sexual relations are openly permitted. Couples who wish to live together are allowed to do so.

In the past: Residents had to obey staff orders and to behave in accordance with staff expectations. "The staff knows best" was axiomatic and arguing was considered disrespectful and manipulative.

Today: The staff is learning to respond to residents' expectations. Residents are taught how to criticize and the staff is taught how to deal with this new, sometimes embarrassing, phenomenon.

In the past: Kfar Tikva was regarded as a traditional institution by staff, parents, and residents. It was financially dependent on monthly fees paid by parents, guardians, or the government. This state of affairs was perceived as a permanent fact of life.

Today: Kfar Tikva's economic independence is increasing. Parents, residents, and staff share the goal of economic independence and self-sufficiency without help from outside sources–a goal shared by every kibbutz in Israel. Today Kfar Tikva is engaged in promoting the participation of its residents in all decision-making processes. Residents have even expressed their desire to participate in meetings of the board of directors, and the Residents' Committee is studying ways in which this could be done. Residents are also learning how the staff should function and how to supervise them. They are learning how to deal promptly with all cases of disrespect or abuse, whether by staff or by residents. In meetings between staff and residents it has been made clear that, in the future, residents will have the authority to admonish, suspend, and even fire staff.

THE QUALITY OF SERVICE AND ACADEMIC COURSES

In the institutional phase of Kfar Tikva, the quality of the service offered to residents was an abstract concept. There was no input from residents (clients) and sometimes even from their families about the quality and sufficiency of services provided. Social workers and psychologists made it clear that the verification of the quality of their services is something that cannot be perceived with immediate results: "Psychotherapy and rehabilitation is an on-going, sometimes long, process." In many cases social workers, psychologists and/or other staff members involved in direct care saw quality (if they saw it at all) as a "philosophical trend" and a "goal on the horizon."

Kfar Tikva worked in the last four years to change the concept of quality of services provided to residents. The process began with a slow but steady approach to Total Quality Management (TQM) and it continued by applying for and receiving the International Standard of Quality ISO 9001, making it one of the first services in the world for people with special needs to receive such recognition. The introduction of the new standards of quality created quite a revolutionary change in the perception of quality provided to the people we treat or who are under our care. Relating to families and residents as clients brought a fast and very perceptible change on the quality of life of the residents. Every complaint from a resident or a parent or even a suggestion of dissatisfaction is immediately put in writing and dealt with by the Quality Committee created in the village. The Quality Committee became a tool for creating change and continuous improvement.

In the institutional period of Kfar Tikva, academic courses such as history, geography, computers or any other class were part of the leisure or educational time of the residents in the village and were restricted to the premises of the village only. In 1992 Kfar Tikva approached Haifa

University's Department of External Studies, which provides non-degree, external academic courses. Kfar Tikva proposed that the University should create similar courses including or especially tailor-made for people with special needs. Haifa's first reaction was resistance. It struck us as surprising that the same academic institution which in its schools of psychology and social work proclaimed that normalization and inclusion are a "must" when considering the life of people with special needs, when it came to "delivering the goods" erected a barrier. This was one of the situations where we felt that we were knocking on doors in the middle of the desert. But of course those doors had neon inscriptions on them: "Normalization and inclusion are taught here."

After some persuasion, Haifa University agreed that a group of 20 people could participate in an academic course of political science. This program was so successful and brought so many positive public relations to Haifa University that the next year, 1993, two more courses were initiated: psychology and computers. Today six courses are taught at Haifa University for people with special needs, including advanced courses in computers, languages, politics, psychology, and art. Kfar Tikva initiated a similar program at the Jezreel College where 20 people are now studying creative writing.

These initiatives created a real inclusion of people with special needs in the wider society and provided an accelerating feeling for the person with special needs who now can stroll the University corridors and use the library and students' cafeteria. Another important result of this project was the relationship created between the traditional students and Kfar Tikva residents, changing some stereotypes and preconceptions and even stigma.

CONCLUSIONS:
LESSONS FOR THE INTERNATIONAL COMMUNITY

Human Beings with Special Needs as Clients

Kfar Tikva is a concept that transcends its geographical position and based on a strong belief in the capacity for growth in every human being. Any institution or service for people with special needs can alter its rules to enable maximum participation. Committees can be formed to deal with all matters concerning everyday life and decisions affecting clients and staff. Clients should participate in planning the service from the beginning and in regular staff and board meetings. Staff and boards only exist by virtue of their clients.

Any institution or service for people with special needs can and must, in our opinion, create the possibility for its residents to live in the community in homes or in apartments in a least-restricted environment. Staff are actually employees of the clients. Why is it that we automatically assume that they have no opinions to express and no authority to exercise regarding staff matters, including salaries, working hours, and work standards? Some people may claim that this is a very risky approach, but risk-taking is inherent in any sincere belief in human beings.

Any service can encourage its clients to exercise choice or participate in choosing recreational and educational programs. Any service can and must respect privacy and freedom of movement. Any service can help its clients understand that the keys to their rooms are theirs only. Generally clients learn this more quickly than the staff. Clients can also learn more quickly that the staff work for them, are directly paid by them, and can be hired and fired by them. Any institution, hostel or group home can decide that sexual life is a natural privilege of human beings.

People with Special Needs as Decision Makers

Any country can encourage the organization of people with special needs. Such an organization could represent its residents, protect their legal rights, and fight against abuse and exploitation. People with special needs, helped by professional advice, should represent other people with special needs. It is essential to create a system to prevent the horrors of the past; 2,000 years ago, the ancient Greeks exterminated people with special needs and, more recently, the Nazis did the same in the name of euthanasia and medical experimentation. These tragedies must not be allowed to reoccur. It is equally important that people with special needs have recourse against future professional decisions that could declare that restrictive institutions are the best solution for them and that people with special needs should go to bed at 8:00 p.m. The only way to avoid closing doors that are only partly open is to give these people power and to teach them how to use it. Keith and Paula Stanvich (1979) expressed the opinion that people with special needs can speak for themselves. The main problem is our lack of readiness to listen.

Training of the Staff

The disappearance of Kfar Tikva as an institution began when some of the staff stopped being deaf to what residents had been saying for a long time. Only in the last few years have residents begun receiving driving licenses to drive cars and tractors, something they asked for 12 years ago. Only recently have they been accepted into the Israeli Army, although this was talked about for years. To what extent is our judgment of the extent of their special needs governed by our refusal to listen? How much of their special needs depends on our preconceptions, stigmatization, and self-fulfilling prophecies? When we first began to work with people with special needs, we thought we had a fair idea of the nature of "special needs." With the passing years we began to forget what we knew, and we still have much to forget. What amazed us was that the less we used what we once had known about people with special needs, the more they grew and developed skills and capabilities. The more we expected from them, the more they responded.

We would suggest that basic training for new staff who will work with people with special needs should require them to forget all that they thought they knew and begin afresh. There are no growth limits for human beings! Ceasing to grow, to learn, and to develop is a decision we can make for ourselves but not for others. If we have reached our limits in helping others grow, someone else must continue our job. Kfar Tikva is a model for assisting people with special needs to achieve a capacity for decision-making instead of having decisions made for them.

AN INSTITUTION IS BECOMING A SETTLEMENT

Kfar Tikva has applied to change its status from an institution to a settlement. Only the Ministry of Interior can carry this out. Since this is a relatively new phenomenon, both residents and staff have the opportunity to learn together how to cope with the legal and technical difficulties involved. This process is helping them to live together on a more equal footing.

As a settlement Kfar Tikva will have the same rights as other settlements such as a bus stop, post office, and access to government budgets for social and cultural development. This will speed up the achievement of economic independence, without which no community can be effective. The transformation of Kfar Tikva from an institution into a settlement will only be complete when legal recognition is attained and economic independence is achieved. In such a framework, it is of the utmost importance that residents hire the staff they need to help them to run their daily lives and that they have the power of decision regarding whether they want to continue living in Kfar Tikva or to move to another community.

As a settlement Kfar Tikva can be the basis for the foundation of other communities. When a new kibbutz is built, the residents of the new settlement live in an older kibbutz for one or two years. After that period they go and settle independently. Kfar Tikva can be the "mother settlement" where a group of the village population, together with a population which does not have special needs, would live together and prepare for settling. The pioneers would move later to their new settlement. In the new community every member would participate equally in the work according to vocational and personal capacities. In these types of settlements, after several years, differences between people formerly labeled people with special needs and those considered normal would diminish. There people with special needs would be a natural and active part of the community growth (Pencovici, 1982).

Our main focus is not to bring people with special needs to the community or to create a community for people with special needs. We shouldn't forget that the community is not a goal but a means to our goal of capacitating people for independence and decision-making (Pencovici & Newman, 1979). Those considered people with special needs have the same right as others to participate in political and social life. It is our obligation to help them understand the society they live in. It is also our obligation to help them understand that change is possible and that conflict is permissible.

AUTHOR NOTE

Arie Pencovici is a social worker. He is the president and C.E.O. of Kfar Tikva since 1975. Initiator of changing the concept of institution (for people with special needs) to their life in the community. Initiator of Kfar Tikva in Brazil and Switzerland. Winner of several awards for work in the field of mental retardation and advocacy for the rights of people with special needs.

REFERENCES

Corcoran, P. (1978). *Integration of independent living into the total rehabilitation process: Annual progress report,* 7 (pp. 60-70). Boston: Medical Rehabilitation Research and Training Center, Tufts-New England Medical Center.

DeJong, G. (1978, November 17). *The movement for independent living: Origins, ideology, and implications for disability research.* Paper presented at the annual meeting of the American Congress of Rehabilitation Medicine, New Orleans, Louisiana.

Pencovici, A. (1982). *The "death" of an institution and the "birth" of a new settlement.* Paper Presented at the 6th International Congress for the Scientific Study of Mental Deficiency (ICSSMD), Toronto.

Pencovici, A., & Newman, E. (1979). *Kfar Tikva: A community model for vocational rehabilitation of the mentally retarded.* Paper presented at the 5th International Congress for Scientific Research of Mental Retardation (IASSMD), Jerusalem.

Stanovich, K., Stanovich, E., & Paul J. (1979). Speaking for themselves: A bibliography of writings by mentally handicapped individuals. *Mental Retardation,* 17(2).

Wolfensberger, W. (1979). *An attempt toward a theology of social integration of devalued/handicapped people.* Information Service of the Religion Division of the American Association on Mental Deficiency (Volume 8, Number 1).

The Project for the Education
of Israeli Children in the Kibbutz Movement

Edna Shoham
Neomi Shiloah

SUMMARY. In Israel there are various settings in which children can be raised if for various reasons they cannot live with their families. This article describes one of these programs, The Project for the Education of Israeli Children (*Mif' al Lehahsharat Yaldei Israel*) (Brashi, 1994), and focuses on the role of the kibbutz movement. The Project is special in that children are placed in foster families (or family homes), offering them not only warmth and love but also the opportunity for a remedial experience of family life in functioning families that provide physical and emotional support. The first part presents a general outline of the Project, and the second part describes the development of the Project in the kibbutz movement: the absorption procedures, the foster families and foster family homes, and the advantages and difficulties of absorbing children within a kibbutz framework. *[Article copies available for a fee from The Haworth Document Delivery Service: 1-800-342-9678. E-mail address: <getinfo@ haworthpressinc.com> Website: <http://www.HaworthPress.com> © 2001 by The Haworth Press, Inc. All rights reserved.]*

KEYWORDS. Foster care, family home, kibbutz education, community integration, residential care

Edna Shoham and Neomi Shiloah are affiliated with Oranim and Haifa University.

[Haworth co-indexing entry note]: "The Project for the Education of Israeli Children in the Kibbutz Movement." Shoham, Edna, and Neomi Shiloah. Co-published simultaneously in *Child & Youth Services* (The Haworth Press, Inc.) Vol. 22, No. 1/2, 2001, pp. 37-53; and: *Innovative Approaches in Working with Children and Youth: New Lessons from the Kibbutz* (ed: Yuval Dror) The Haworth Press, Inc., 2001, pp. 37-53. Single or multiple copies of this article are available for a fee from The Haworth Document Delivery Service [1-800-342-9678, 9:00 a.m. - 5:00 p.m. (EST). E-mail address: getinfo@haworthpressinc.com].

In Israel there are various settings in which children can be raised if for various reasons they cannot live in their natural families (Arieli & Feuerstein, 1987; Jaffe, 1983). This article describes one of these programs, The Project for the Education of Israeli Children (*Mif' al Lehahsharat Yaldei Israel*), with a focus on the role of the kibbutz movement.

This project is one of the leading Israeli institutions in Israel dealing with boarding school education for young children. It accepts boys and girls from nursery school age up to the 7th grade, and they are educated in the Project's institutions until the end of junior high school. Then they go on to other programs or return to their homes, if conditions permit. The Project is unique in Israel in that it places the children in families (or family homes), offering them not only warmth and love but also the opportunity for a remedial experience of family life in functioning families that provide physical and emotional support.

HISTORICAL BACKGROUND

The Project for the Education of Israeli Children was established in 1943 upon the initiative of Reha Freier.[1] From 1943 to 1973 it placed children from families in distress in kibbutz families. The aim of the Project was to identify neglected children of primary school age and place them in kibbutzim. The children were integrated within the kibbutz children's society and the local school (Blitz, 1994).

In 1973, the Ministry of Education adopted the Project and provided funding that enabled more difficult children to return[2] to school. These were youth who had dropped out of the educational system and whose parents were unable to safeguard their physical and mental health for various reasons: death, disease, drugs, crime, divorce, etc. As a result of this support the Project was expanded to three additional settings outside the kibbutz, including:

1. *Foster families outside the kibbutz.* Foster families living in towns, cooperative villages, or villages raise up to four children within their own family and home. These are children who are in need of a great deal of attention. They may never have experienced real family life, and they are in need of a warm, supportive atmosphere and a model of daily life in a functioning family.
2. *Foster family homes.* These homes take in 10 to 15 children and operate according to the model of a family unit; they are autono-

mous in the satisfaction of their needs and function like any family with many children. The children are in school in the morning and come home in the afternoon. They help at home, do their homework, and play like other children in large families.

3. *Children's homes and children's villages.* The children's home consists of 3 to 7 groups of family units and the children's village of 8 to 20 such groups. In each family there is a couple, acting as parents. Three or four children share a room that is spacious and complete with furniture and toys; the living room and kitchen are shared by the family group. The children's daily life resembles that of an ordinary family: They go to school in the community, come home in the afternoon for social activities and for study, and participate in various courses, youth movement activities, and enrichment lessons. They help prepare supper, watch television, and "the parents" or other children help them with their homework (Nevo, 1994; Steinitz, 1986).

As we can see, the three models that have developed on the basis of the initial kibbutz model share certain characteristics. The family home is based on the concept of foster parents: The children are able to grow up in a supportive family environment, they develop within a larger and diverse children's group with the benefit of supportive, informal education, and they are assisted in their studies and in coping with social life.

THE EDUCATIONAL CONCEPTION

The educational work is based on the teachings of Korczak (Lifton, 1988) and on the kibbutz, foster-family home model. The main educational principles stemming from Korczak's philosophy are:

1. The educators must serve as models for the children in their actions and reactions: They must be honest, consistent, devoted.
2. The educators in the boarding school are to replace the parents; they must treat the children as though they are their own, be aware of their needs and seek to satisfy them, and understand and help solve their problems.
3. The educators should foster the children's latent ability and talents and treat them and their opinions and desires with respect. Above all they should love the children unconditionally.

4. In addition to love and empathy for the children, the educators should develop mutual trust between the children.
5. The educators must prepare the children for adult life. They must foster their independence and responsibility and teach them work habits and manners (Kahana, 1994).

ADMISSION AND ORGANIZATIONAL PROCEDURES

Children are admitted into the program according to the following criteria: (a) Children suffering from neglect and rejection in their families, usually children from families in a state of economic and cultural deprivation; (b) children from families in which one or both parents suffer from a physical or mental illness, preventing them from functioning as a supportive family; (c) children from families in which one or both parents are criminals; (d) children from one-parent families who do not provide for the child's basic needs; and (e) children from families where there is physical, mental, or sexual violence (Riaz, 1994).

Kibbutz movements on their own choose criteria for the absorption of the children. The most important one is finding a kibbutz family willing to take in the child and treat him or her as one of their own. Unlike children in the other programs, those absorbed in the kibbutzim remain there until the age of 18 when they finished secondary school and joined the army, and they often returned to the kibbutz after their army service. Another usual precondition was that the children would be at grade level in the relevant kibbutz class and would fit into the group of children that would absorb them. Today kibbutzim take in children aged 6 to 14 with an average or higher level of intelligence when all attempts at rehabilitation within their home community have failed.

The absorption of children on kibbutzim is complex, because kibbutz society in general and its educational framework in particular are very different from anything the child has known. While having to get used to their foster families, the children must also be part of the children's society. This is a group of children who have lived, played, and learned together for a long time–throughout their childhood. This combination of entering a strange family, a cohesive group of children, and a community whose way of life is different from anything the children have known makes it hard for them to adapt and to forge their own identities, and they have to make a great effort in order to become successfully integrated (Shuki, 1995).

The Project has two absorption programs in the kibbutzim: Foster families and the foster family home.

THE FOSTER FAMILIES

Kibbutz families are willing to serve as foster families for various reasons.

1. They wish to help children in distress. Amir said:

> We saw on the kibbutz bulletin board a circular sent by the Project, trying to interest the members in adopting a child as a foster family. At that stage in our lives we had not planned to take care of a strange child. It was a spontaneous decision. We thought about it while on holiday: We love children, so why shouldn't we do something for someone in such need of help and support. We told our children about it and they agreed.

2. Some families wanted to have more children and at the same time to help children from families in distress. Uri said:

> My wife and I wanted to enlarge our family. We had two sons and we wanted another. We also felt we should help someone in need–a child in trouble. By chance we read an article in the newspaper that they are looking for foster parents for a boy of 9. We contacted the author of the article and through her the biological father of the child. After the father had agreed to our proposal, we turned to the Project and asked the kibbutz to arrange all the formalities. We told our children about it and we made the decision together with them. We met a nice child who seemed well developed and we were all happy to have him with us in the family.

3. Other families whose children had grown up said they still felt young and able to bring up more children. Nurit said:

> The Project's administrators asked the local school to accept a few children. The school was interested in enlarging the number of pupils and suggested I take one of them. I agreed, since my own chil-

dren were grown up and had left home and I love children–they are cheerful, boisterous and full of life. But I asked for two girls; they would become friends and it would make it easier for them to cope with the difficulties of adapting to a new life. I didn't ask the rest of my family for their opinion, I just told them after making the decision. Our first meeting was very moving: Two thin, pathetic-looking little girls who didn't know anyone or each other. Sad little girls; the smaller one was shy and didn't say a word, the older one spoke a little more.

4. Some were second marriage couples who knew they would not have children of their own and wanted to bring up a child together or couples who had children of the same sex and wanted to have a child of the other sex.

A woman came to me and told me they were too old to have a child of their own but wanted to have a child at home who belonged to both of them, to enable them to share the joys and difficulties of bringing up a child together. She said they felt young enough to cope with the problems and were waiting impatiently for the child.

5. Others were kibbutz families in which one or both parents had been educated on a kibbutz within the framework of the Project and considered it their obligation to provide a home for other children in the same plight. They emphasized their appreciation of the Project and of what had been done for them while growing up on a kibbutz.
6. Some requests of kibbutz members to take in a child came from families whose child had died, and they wished to have another.

On the kibbutz the responsibility for the child's upbringing is not only the family's. All the kibbutz institutions participate in the decision and share the responsibility for the absorption, upkeep, and education of the child. This has many advantages. However, it sometimes causes difficulties in the relationship between the family and the kibbutz due to problems the child may cause. The Project's supervisors visit the kibbutz in order to talk to the foster family and provide guidance. If psychological problems arise, the family can turn to the Project's head psychologist for assistance and guidance. Also, refresher courses are organized for the foster families every year, including a course for all the new foster families in the country, and regional courses for all the families.

In spite of the support and assistance the foster families receive from institutions outside and inside the kibbutz, problems do occur and the primary responsibility for coping falls on the foster family. These problems include learning difficulties, personal difficulties, communication troubles, and relationship problems.

The Children's Learning Problems

They come deprived of proper schooling and with low motivation, detrimental to their progress at school. Nurit said:

> The girls did not think study important. Being socially accepted was more important for them, and so they invested a great deal of effort to this end. I was always having to go to the school and fight for them to prevent them from being expelled from school.

Uri said:

> He had many learning problems, especially at first with reading and writing. He also had difficulties later and was unable to finish 12 years of school. He found it difficult to pull himself together and cope with his studies.

Personal Problems

The transition from the biological family to a foster family and kibbutz society caused the children a great deal of stress.
Nurit said:

> After six months one of the girls used to follow me like a little dog. Their being two years old didn't help. She didn't speak and only clung to me all the time.

Uri recalled:

> At first the boy would only eat schnitzel, chips, and clear soup–nothing else. The day his biological father died he sat alone in the hospital and no one from his biological family came to be with him. My heart ached for him when I saw him so lonely.

Amir had a similar story:

> We live in a religious kibbutz and the child came from a secular family. He experienced a conflict between two world views. In order to resolve it, he wore a skullcap and did not travel on the Sabbath. When he went home to his own family he took off the skullcap, went to the beach on Saturday, and traveled by bus.

Difficulties Connected to Communication with the Biological Family

Usually there is little close contact, for two reasons: The foster families want to draw a clear line between the child's life on the kibbutz and the outside, as explained by Nurit:

> I realized there must be a distance between myself and the biological family so they won't tell me what to do, and the child will not use the two families in a manipulative way.

Sometimes the biological family is not really interested in keeping in touch with the foster family, trying to convince themselves that the child is well looked after and there is no need to worry about him. Uri said:

> Though we tried hard to persuade his biological family that it was important they come and keep up the contact with him, they hardly ever came and they didn't show an interest in him. After the death of his father no one came to visit him (except his grandmother once). The contact with them was very complicated in spite of all our efforts to keep it up.

Amir said that contact with the parents, especially with the mother (there was hardly any contact with the father), was problematic. For instance,

> Once when we had visitors, his biological mother suddenly rang up and said to the child, "Tell your foster father to contact me tomorrow at 9:00." This was to fix up when and where she would tell us what to do. When she found out that the child gets presents from the grandparents of our own children, she told him that he also has grandparents (which he didn't know), and they would also bring him presents. She seemed to be competing for the child's love.

Problems Stemming from Possible Harm to Relationships Within the Foster Family

The foster families describe how at first the children's arrival upset to some extent the delicate balance that exists in every family. For instance, Eileen (the biological daughter of a foster family) said:

> I had the feeling that mother is giving more to the adopted children than to me. I left the kibbutz, I had children, and I wanted mother to help me. I thought that she wasn't helping me enough because of the adopted girls. It drove me crazy that they were always sitting and watching television. Whenever I called, one of the girls would lift the receiver and it would upset me–Why does mother let them use the phone?–and I would say coldly, "Call mother."

Dolly, the second biological daughter in the same family, adds that she did not let them enter her room. "I was the youngest in the family, I thought I deserved everything, and suddenly they came and took a lot of mother's attention away from me."

Today both daughters say that the adopted daughters belong to the family and all the resentment and the differences have disappeared. Uri also mentioned that

> . . . something happened to the dynamics within the family when the child arrived. Suddenly a strange child is around at home, and we must pay attention to what we are saying and wearing, someone is using the toilet, resting, and so on. Suddenly the family intimacy has been tampered with; after all there is a difference between your own child and the adopted one.

In recent years fewer families have been willing to take in children. In 1989 there were 130 children in 70 kibbutzim (Veerman, 1989). In 1995 there were 70 children in 35 kibbutzim (Shuki, 1995). In 1998 there were 50 children in 22 kibbutzim. The reasons are to be found in the change processes taking place in kibbutz society. During the first years of the existence of the kibbutzim, it repudiated the importance of the family. It assumed important functions traditionally fulfilled by the family such as bringing up children and providing services such as laundry, food, and health care. In the course of time a more individualistic approach took over in the kibbutz movement, and the members and their families were given greater responsibility and authority. Dar (1998) describes it in this way:

> Until 1984 the kibbutz society appeared confident in its collective identity, its strength as a social movement, its multigenerational continuity, its organizational efficiency and its economic stability. It has taken only a few years for it to become confused, anxious about its future, for its self-image to deteriorate . . . Many kibbutzim are concentrating their efforts on the rehabilitation of their economic base and are preoccupied by their search for new directions . . . The spirit of utopian endeavor has waned and a moderate individualism has replaced the communal ethos together with a great increase in the role of the family within the community and in its importance for the individual. (p. 7)

Dar (1998) points out that these social changes are reflected in kibbutz education and influence it. As the family has grown more powerful and its educational role has expanded (including having the children sleep at home), the community's responsibility for education has diminished and the power and authority of its educational agents has declined. This process has contributed to a change in the educational approach: Rather than focusing on the child as embodying the hope for the community's future, the focus is on the child (of the parents) as an individual whose unique needs should be met and abilities developed as far as possible. (See also Bar-Lev, 1996; Ben-Rafael, 1996; Rosner & Goetz, 1996.)

Formerly, the children would spend only a few hours a day with their foster parents and the rest of the time with their own age-group. Today they spend most of their spare time with their foster families, which is a burden for the family and makes the whole process of absorption more difficult (Dar, 1995; Israelowitz, 1986). The children staying with their parents, economic difficulties, privatization, and the individual taking center stage make it very hard to find a family willing to take in another child. With the children living at home, all aspects of the parents' married life together with the human relationships within the family are thus revealed to another person (Shuki, 1995). This new situation, along with fewer foster families available, has led to the implementation of the idea of the foster family home on kibbutz.

THE FOSTER FAMILY HOME

The first foster family home was set up in 1995 in Kibbutz Meirav in northern Israel, a small religious kibbutz with a young adult population. There were several reasons for this choice:

1. Religious kibbutz society is more ideologically conscious and has preserved more of the communal aspects than the secular kibbutz movement. The changes it is undergoing in various spheres are slower than in secular kibbutz society (Bar-Lev, 1996). Therefore the kibbutz agreed to undertake responsibilities to help out children in need of a home.
2. The number of members in Kibbutz Meirav is small, so there are few children. Absorbing children in this way helps the kibbutz to overcome the resulting difficulties and enables it to create a larger children's society.
3. The project pays the salary of the couple working in the family home and so provides jobs and livelihood for two members. In the family home in Meirav there are 10 children aged 5 to 12. Since it was difficult to find a married couple among the kibbutz members–a couple providing a good model of married life for children coming from problematic homes–the kibbutz assigned to the family home two people who are not married: A full-time housemother and a half-time educator.

Unlike a foster family, the mixed age-group makes it possible to accept siblings. All the children have families in the kibbutz who host them twice a week and on Sabbath mornings (usually the parents of a child who has befriended the new child). However, their lives are centered on the foster family home. In the afternoons they participate in clubs together with the kibbutz children. Sometimes these are organized by the kibbutz and sometimes by the members in charge of the family home. The dynamics within the group show that after the children have been absorbed, they in turn absorb the newcomers. The children are integrated with the kibbutz children in their studies and social life; they do not form a separate group.

Like the kibbutz children, these children study at the regional school together with the children from religious kibbutzim and moshavim in the area. It is a comparatively large school of 850 children which makes it possible to offer all the children various programs facilitating their absorption and speedy integration. Indeed, all the children suffering from learning and emotional deprivation when they came have been able to close the gaps in the course of time, each according to his or her level and progress.

The second foster family home was set up in September, 1997, in Kibbutz Saad, a relatively large religious kibbutz in central Israel. Unlike Meirav, the team working in the family home is a married couple. Since no kibbutz family was willing to play this role, a family was hired for the purpose. This caused tensions between the members and the hired couple who was unfamiliar with the kibbutz system and unaware of the extent to which they could use kibbutz services and get help from kibbutz functionaries and institutions in a better and more efficient way for the benefit of the children. The kibbutz also appears to be less aware of its obligations to the children of the family home if the foster parents are not members.

Ten children were accepted, including three pairs of siblings. The children learn in the small local school, which makes it more difficult for the school to organize their absorption and for the children to become integrated, because the learning options are restricted. After one year, there were still problems in the study and social spheres.

In 1998 an attempt was made to get secular kibbutzim involved in setting up foster family homes. Negotiations are in progress with two kibbutzim where there are married couples willing to take responsibility for a foster family home. Secular kibbutzim have two obvious advantages over religious kibbutzim: There are more secular kibbutzim, so more options are available for absorbing children in this way, and the secular kibbutzim provide a suitable framework for absorbing children from secular families.

SUCCESSES AND DIFFICULTIES
IN KIBBUTZ ABSORPTION OF CHILDREN

The absorption of children within the kibbutz framework–in foster families or family homes–has a number of advantages over other forms of absorption:

1. In spite of the changes that have taken place, kibbutz society still ascribes to certain basic values: mutual help, social justice, solidarity, and partnership.
2. The kibbutz cares for people even when economic resources have been privatized. It provides food, laundry, study, school materials, informal education, and medical help for all the children and adults of all ages. No sick person will remain unattended and no child will go hungry, whatever the economic situation of the kibbutz.
3. It is less of a closed society than it used to be, but it still has the advantages of a closed society, providing greater security to the child and to the family. There is no fear of violence or falling into troubles.
4. The openness of kibbutz society to its environment and its interaction with it facilitate absorption, since young "kibbutzniks" are now exposed to various types of people, to different opinions and cultures, and no longer relate to the children coming from outside as strangers different and difficult to associate with but rather as people like those they meet such as kibbutz residents who are not members, figures familiar from the media, and so on.
5. The foster families devote themselves to their role without seeking to benefit financially or for other irrelevant reasons, but because they believe that it is the way to help the children and society. This increases the trust of the biological parents and the institutions dealing with the children. If problems arise in the foster family, kibbutz society will help the children and solve the problems. The community provides assistance to the children and the families in case of need.
6. The biological families prefer to hand over their children to kibbutzim, considering them as a high-caliber, supportive society. Moreover, adoption of the child in a kibbutz is seen by the biological family as integration in another, different society. Adoption in a town increases the biological family's feelings of failure, since it is not a case of a different social environment but merely belonging to a different family.

Besides the many advantages, two main difficulties are clearly evident:

1. The decrease in the number of kibbutz families willing to take in children. Kibbutz members get tired of absorbing newcomers, of contributing to society, and of coping with difficulties over and above those inherent in their daily lives, especially the economic difficulties.

2. Social-cultural difficulties. Children entering a foster family in a town usually remain within the social and cultural framework familiar to them. On kibbutzim they have to cope with a very different way of life and culture in addition to the difficulties in becoming integrated in a largely homogeneous group of children who share a common past.

CONCLUSION

What can be considered as successful absorption of children and adolescents on kibbutzim?

Until 10 years ago, absorption was considered successful when young people, brought up on kibbutz within the framework of the Project, joined the kibbutz as members after their army service. Veerman (1989) reported that of the 75 replies he received, 59 people are still living on kibbutz. Veerman considered this proof of successful absorption and integration of the children in the kibbutzim.

Today the attitude is far more complex. Amalia, in charge of the Project in the kibbutzim, considers the children spending almost 10 years on kibbutz as a proof of success. Hardly any of these children leave, while among children in children's homes in town, 12% leave for other programs when going from the primary school to junior high, and 30% leave when going on to high school.

Amalia also considers it a success when the children are able to complete 12 years of schooling and join the army. She tells about a survey carried out in 1992 that examined the performance of these children in the school-leaving exams. Many of the graduates completed successfully all the requirements of the school-leaving certificate, a very unusual and impressive success even when compared on a national scale to the well-established population. In her opinion this is due to the careful screening of the children before they are admitted to the kibbutz (because of the complexity of their absorption on kibbutz, mainly children with learning potential and who are socially suitable are accepted), to their tremendous motivation to succeed in spite of the difficulties, and also the help and support they receive in kibbutz society.

How is success defined by the foster families? Nurit considers it an achievement

. . . that the girls have become a part of the family. They participate in all the important occasions such as festivals, parties, trips, and so on. They feel they are a part of the family. They always remember to buy presents and they write loving letters. My biological children also benefited. They understand what it means to give and to receive and what happiness this brings. The moment my biological children accepted the girls as a part of the family, I considered it a great achievement of mine.

For Uri, success lies in the fact that,

The boy (now in the army) feels comfortable and confident about coming to us whenever and for as long as he wants to. He knows we shall always welcome him and help him. In spite of the clashes we sometimes have, he always comes home on leave and feels free to do here whatever he feels like.

Amir considers it a success that the child will grow up and won't be on welfare; he will contribute to society and feel good about himself and about what he does. He sums up:

One of my friends told me that the adoption of these children can be seen as a great achievement by the family and by the kibbutz society in which it lives. Such achievements seem to provide a justification for the whole of the kibbutz endeavor.

How do the graduates of the Project sum up the period of their life on kibbutz?

The years I spent on kibbutz were the most important ones and the best thing that happened to me: years of continual learning with many opportunities to extend my horizons in any direction I wished. I studied classical and modern dance, played various musical instruments, went on trips all over the country. Happy years of study together with extensive social and cultural activity in which I participated and certainly played a role. (Nevo, 1994, p. 175)

Sometimes I sit and think, "How did I get here and what would have happened if I had stayed at home with my own parents?" And I think it was a step that saved me from a hard life. Who knows where I might have ended up if I had stayed in that place which has left me with bad memories to this day, even though I was only a small child at the time and hardly understood what life is about. Believe me, I want to thank you so much; the trouble is that I simply don't know how to say it. (Nevo, 1994, p. 167)

NOTE

1. Reha Freier was born in 1892 in Germany and died in 1984 in Israel. She began the work of bringing Jewish youth from Germany to kibbutzim (*Aliat Hanoar*), thus saving their lives. She immigrated to Israel in 1941.

AUTHOR NOTES

Edna Shoham is Dr. (PhD), Senior Teacher of Education, in the University of Haifa and Oranim. Her specializations are history teaching, teacher education and curriculum studies. She is a member of kibbutz Yifat.

Neomi Shiloah is Dr. (PhD), Teacher of Education, in the University of Haifa and Oranim. Her specializations are history, history teaching and teacher education.

REFERENCES

Arieli, M., & Feuerstein, R. (1987). The two-fold care organization: On combining the group and foster care. *Child and Youth Care Quarterly, 16*(3), 168-184.

Bar-Lev, M. (1996). Secondary school education in the religious kibbutz–between collectivism and individualism. *Studies on the Rebirth of Israel, 6*, 402-425. (In Hebrew).

Ben-Rafael, A. (1996). *Not a complete revolution.* Efal: Yad Tabenkin. (In Hebrew).

Blitz, E. (1994). The project for the education of Israeli children, from 1969 to 1979. In M. Nevo (Ed.), *The Project for the Education of Israeli Children, Jubilee Book.* Jerusalem: Ministry of Education, 209-210. (In Hebrew).

Brashi, A. (1994). The Project for the education of Israeli children–what next? In M. Nevo (Ed.), *The Project for the Education of Israeli Children, Jubilee Book.* Jerusalem: Ministry of Education, 2-4. (In Hebrew).

Dar, Y. (1995). Kibbutz education: A sociological account. *Journal of Moral Education, 24(3)*, 225-144.

Dar, Y. (1998). *Education in the changing kibbutz: Sociological and psychological aspects.* Jerusalem: Magnes and Yad Tabenkin. (In Hebrew).

Israelowitz, R. (1986). *The influence of child sleeping arrangement on selected aspects of kibbutz life.* Efal: Yad-Tabenkin.

Jaffe, E. (1983). *Israelis in institutions: Studies in child placement, practices and policy.* New York: Gordon and Beatch.

Kahana, Y. (1994). A new stage in the development of the Project for the education of Israeli children 1973-1978. In M. Nevo (Ed.), *The Project for the Education of Israeli Children, Jubilee Book.* Jerusalem: Ministry of Education, 211-214. (In Hebrew).

Lifton, B. J. (1988). *The king of children: A biography of Janusz Korczak*. NY: Farrar, Straus, & Giroux.

Nevo, M. (Ed.). (1994). *The Project for the Education of Israeli Children, Jubilee Book*. Jerusalem: Ministry of Education. (In Hebrew).

Riaz, H. (1994). Admission and placement of the children in the Project. In M. Nevo (Ed.), *The Project for the Education of Israeli Children, Jubilee Book* (pp. 61-63). Jerusalem: Ministry of Education. (In Hebrew).

Rosner, M., & Goetz, S. (1996). *The kibbutz at a time of change*. Tel-Aviv: Hakibbutz Hameuhad and Haifa University. (In Hebrew).

Shuki, A. (1995). The Project for the education of Israeli children. *Education Pages*, 7, 32-34. (In Hebrew).

Steinitz, R. (1986). The foster family-home. In Y. Kashti & M. Arieli (Eds.), *People in institutions: The Israeli scene*. London: Freund Pub.

Veerman, P. E. (1989). Foster families in kibbutzim. *Adoption & Fostering, 13* (2), 48-52.

Educating Youth Groups
in Kibbutz Communities:
The Interests of the Kibbutz

Simha Shlasky

SUMMARY. Studying people processing settings might elucidate ways by which hegemonic groups define images and knowledge about people in care and thus construct their own and others' social identities. Since 1934 many kibbutzim have accommodated groups of adolescents for a period of 2 to 6 years of education within their communities ("Kibbutz Youth Groups"). These groups consisted of immigrant or socially disadvantaged adolescents and were organized and supervised by public agencies, especially *Youth Aliyah*. *[Article copies available for a fee from The Haworth Document Delivery Service: 1-800-342-9678. E-mail address: <getinfo@ haworthpressinc.com> Website: <http://www.HaworthPress.com> © 2001 by The Haworth Press, Inc. All rights reserved.]*

KEYWORDS. Kibbutz education, youth work, Youth Aliyah, Foucault, social construction of identity, ethics, youth services, youth policy, groupwork

This residential program was researched, until now, mainly from an educational point of view, e.g., to what extent students adjusted to the

---

Simha Shlasky is affiliated with the Israeli extension of the University of Derby (UK).

[Haworth co-indexing entry note]: "Educating Youth Groups in Kibbutz Communities: The Interests of the Kibbutz." Shlasky, Simha. Co-published simultaneously in *Child & Youth Services* (The Haworth Press, Inc.) Vol. 22, No. 1/2, 2001, pp. 55-74; and: *Innovative Approaches in Working with Children and Youth: New Lessons from the Kibbutz* (ed: Yuval Dror) The Haworth Press, Inc., 2001, pp. 55-74. Single or multiple copies of this article are available for a fee from The Haworth Document Delivery Service [1-800-342-9678, 9:00 a.m. - 5:00 p.m. (EST). E-mail address: getinfo@haworthpressinc.com].

55

kibbutz way of life and identified with its ideals. Interests of the kibbutz in admitting and educating those groups, as well as the influence of these youth groups' presence on the kibbutz as a community and as a political entity were not investigated.

Analysis of the discourse of kibbutz agents indicates that regarding themselves as pioneers in a social and national mission, the kibbutz members treated the youth groups' students as "Others," as different in regard to their motives of immigration and the culture they represented. Defining the identity of the youth groups' students as "Others" served the construction of kibbutz members' own identity as pioneers and elite.

The kibbutz youth group (KYG) is a residential, educational program formed especially for youth from outside the kibbutz who have left or prefer to leave their family homes; they are brought to a kibbutz community for several years of residential education. Each group consists of a few dozen youths[1] of the same age group, between 12 and 17 years old. Until 1996, they were organized, financed, and supervised by the Youth Aliyah department of the Jewish Agency. The Israeli Ministry of Education is now the sponsor of the program. This educational program was founded in 1933 as a joint program of the Jewish Agency and the kibbutz movements for rescuing Jewish boys and girls from Nazi persecutions. The first group arrived in the country in February 1934, and since then more than 50,000 youths (Shalom, 1982) have been educated this way.

The educational program consists of formal academic studies, informal social activities, and work in the kibbutz business or service. Over the years the proportion of time devoted to academics has increased at the expense of work. In the past and now in special cases, the group studied together outside and inside school. The length of stay for each group in the program varied from 2 to 6 years and depended also on the age of admittance of group members.

In most cases, the group formally belongs to the kibbutz but resides in its own quarters separated from the children of Kibbutz members. Families of the kibbutz community "adopt" every boy and girl of the group, allowing access to kibbutz community life through work, meals, and general events of a cultural and recreational nature.

Each new youth group cohort must be accepted by the kibbutz; thus the KYG is not a continual program in any particular kibbutz. A new KYG is not accepted before the old one is finished.

Staff–usually kibbutz members–is assigned specially for each group. In the past staff were not professionals; eventually professional teachers were introduced, but the day-to-day care is provided by staff members such as the *Metapelet* (the house mother) and the *Madrich* (who is in charge of the informal activities). They are not professionals and they often change during the group's period of education.

This program differs from a typical residential school in that the whole community–its entire population and ways of life–is the socializing influence. The youths' activities are interwoven with regular kibbutz life, and at the end of the program the graduates are generally expected to incorporate some of these lifestyle elements and ideals or even join a kibbutz. This feature of the relations between the kibbutz community and the KYG was described at a very early stage of its existence and produced the term "educating communities" (Tzizling, 1939).

For many years the educational goal was to prepare the graduates to become new kibbutz members who in turn would found new kibbutzim or join existing ones, usually the one in which they were educated. However, in the last two decades there has been no real expectation that graduates will join a kibbutz, and the objectives have been defined instead as socializing for good citizenship and better integration into the mainstream of Israeli society (Gottesmann, 1987).

Presently, 65 years after it was founded, the program seems to be slowly dying. In the early 1990s there were fewer than 1,000 youth compared to more than 7,000 in the peak years at the end of the 1940s, when the general kibbutz population was about 40% of its present size. The question as to what kept the program alive for more than 60 years is no less significant than why it is dying.

THE METHOD OF THIS STUDY

Many surveys and studies about the KYG have investigated educational aspects of the program. The majority have concentrated on the youths' adjustment to the framework or to the kibbutz life system and ideology,[2] while others studied the process of education[3] and some of its products.[4]

The main issue of this study is different, because its focus is the significance of the KYG for the kibbutz. First, what were the interests of the kibbutz in admitting these youths to be educated on its premises? Second, what can be learned about the way the collective identity of the kibbutz members and students was constructed through the discourse of kibbutz members–especially its leaders and educators–about KYGs?

There are three basic differences between this approach and former studies:

1. The subject of this study is the "educating community" rather than the KYG itself;
2. The political rather than the educational aspects of action is the focus of interest;
3. Unlike previous works, the kibbutz is not regarded as an established community that undertakes to acculturate and socialize groups of children in need and absorb them into its stable life system; it is instead regarded as a developing and changing community that experiences new patterns of life, reflects upon its identity, and is concerned as to its position within the political environment.

Based on this last contention, it is claimed here that absorbing KYGs was regarded as a means for recruiting new members, as a means for establishing the kibbutz movement's aspirations for a leading political position within the Jewish community in Palestine and the State of Israel, and taking part in the socialization of a group of young people was an opportunity for examining and consolidating kibbutz members' identity. In each phase of kibbutz development a different aspect was stressed, and different content was given to each aspect.

The study is based on a "discourse analysis" of addresses, speeches, debates, and written materials of kibbutz educators and its political leaders. Discourse analysis, as defined by Potter (1997),

> emphasizes the way versions of the world, of society, events and inner psychological worlds are produced in discourse. On the one hand, this leads to a concern with participants' constructions and how they are accomplished and undermined; and on the other, it leads to a recognition of the constructed and contingent nature of researchers' own versions of the world. Indeed, it treats realism, whether developed by participants or researchers, as a rhetorical production that can itself be decomposed and studied.

> Discourse analysis has an analytical commitment to studying discourse as *texts and talk in social practices* . . . analysis of discourse becomes, then, analysis of what people do. One theme that is particularly emphasized here is the rhetorical or argumentative orga-

nization of talk and texts; claims and versions are constructed to undermine alternatives. (p. 146) (emphasis in the original)

According to Fisk's (1998, p. 371) description:

A discourse analyst studies utterances in order to understand how the potential of the linguistic system can be activated when it intersects at its moments of use with a social system . . . So the cultural analyst studies instances of culture in order to understand both the system that structures "the whole way of life" and the ways of living that people devise within it.

As indicated by Foucault (1972), discourse can be used to differentiate, to divide, and to set power relations; discourse in itself is a means of forming reality. The discursive practices for Foucault, as Dreyfus and Rabinow (1982, p. xx) indicate, "are distinguished from the speech acts of everyday life" by being said by experts "when they are speaking as experts."

KIBBUTZ AND YOUTH GROUP RELATIONSHIPS

Three main periods can be identified in the history of KYGs, according to the different kinds of youths admitted in each period. The first is from the 1930s until the declaration of the State of Israel in 1948. Most youth arrived without their parents and then with World War II, most were refugees. The second period was the 1950s and the 1960s when most of the students were immigrants who arrived with their families, many from Moslem countries. The third period extends through the 1970s and the 1980s when most of the students were Israeli-born, disadvantaged youth. Political and social developments caused the change of population.

The First Period: 1934 to 1948

The main political events of this period were World War II, the Holocaust, the struggle against British rule for free Jewish immigration, the growing national conflict between the Jewish and the Arab communities, and the consolidation of the Labor movement's domination in the Jewish community. Most of the youths admitted to KYGs in those years were boys and girls rescued from Europe. Most lost their families in the Holocaust.

Political Aspect. The common enterprise of the kibbutz movements[5]–educating large groups of immigrant youth brought by the Jewish agency–was bound to have political significance in the dynamic Jewish society of Palestine. Several aims of this enterprise are present in the discourse of kibbutz leaders: rescue of children from persecutions in Europe, recruitment of potential kibbutz members, political mobilization of the immigrant youth, and experiencing whole community life when kibbutz families had no younger generation of their own.

Rescue of Children from Persecutions

The KYG was regarded as the main and best absorption program for youth who emigrated from Germany after the Nazis came to power and for those who survived the Nazi occupation of Europe. The kibbutz regarded itself as a major partner in this national, lifesaving enterprise, which corresponded with the Zionist hopes for the future of Jews. The emphasis was on collective and national goals as well as on saving individuals.

Less than a year after the arrival from Germany of the first KYG, one of the leaders of *Hever Ha'kvutzot* (one of the kibbutz movements) wrote:

> Thousands of Hebrew children face decay if they are not organized to make *Aliyah* [immigrate] to *Eretz Israel* [Palestine]. The rescue of these youth is one of the most important enterprises in the present era. The kibbutzim were the first to absorb these youths. (Baratz, 1935, p. 6)

In the middle of the war, Tabenkin (1942), the leader of *Hakibbutz Hameuhad* (another kibbutz movement), said:

> Multitudes of children, tens and hundreds of thousands who became orphans all over the countries of exile . . . are going to come to us. And the youths that will make *Aliyah* will also be among the builders and the fighters. Our face is to the future–we look forward to this *orphan* who has to become a *working person, a farmer, a laborer and a combatant* . . . it means expanding our settlement . . . . (emphasis in the original)

Although the rescue of children is mentioned, the reinforcement of Jewish settlement as well as the change in vocation and career of the saved children is emphasized. One of the leaders of *Hever Ha'kvutzot* wrote that, "This land, the farm, the group, the working society . . . have released them of the chains of their homeland and subjected them to the new values" (Umansky, 1939, p. 70).

Recruitment of Potential Kibbutz Members

The KYG was regarded as an important source of new recruits for the kibbutz way of life and for accomplishing kibbutz objectives (Landshut, 1944). The British restrictions on immigration started in the mid-1930s, and afterwards the Holocaust destroyed the main source for new kibbutz members, namely, graduates of the East-European Zionist youth movements and members of *Hachalutz* (The Pioneer) movement. KYGs were regarded as a replacement for them. "They continue the chain of building and creating, form new enterprises and reinforce the existing ones. This situation raises the immigrant youth to the level of a vital human reserve for the settlement enterprise in this country" (Umansky, 1939, p. 70).

The flattering phrasing cannot conceal the main interest of the kibbutz movement in accepting youth, and the reality that no choice was given to their members in deciding on the place and kind of education they would be given (Landshut, 1944). In more blunt words, an educational leader of another kibbutz movement says:

> In the present situation of our Movement, when the [Youth] Movement here in the country and the KYGs are the only reserve of the *Kibbutz Ha'rtzi*, the needs of the Movement alone will be accounted. The KYGs have to be ready to move in any path that the Movement find it necessary at a certain moment. (Levant, 1940, p. 11)

The KYG was a means of enhancing the political power of the Labor and Kibbutz Movements within the Jewish community as well as with the Jewish community as a whole in its conflict with the Arab community about national hegemony. In April, 1944, when the prospects of absorbing many refugee children after the war became more concrete, Yaacov Hazan, one of the political leaders of *Ha'kibbutz Ha'rtzi*, said:

> The future of the Jewish community depends on this immigration.
> The 150,000 children that are due to come will determine the
> shape of the Jewish community, of our movement, and of the
> whole kibbutz movement in the future. And our values, the values of
> Socialist-Zionism, will be determined by our ability to absorb and ed-
> ucate the youth that is going to come to us. (Hazan, 1984, p. 4)

In this text and in many others, the education of KYGs is openly spo-
ken of as a strategy for political recruitment and acquiring power. In a po-
litically mobilized society such as the Jewish Palestinian community at
that time, this kind of discourse was not exceptional; it defined the absorption of KYGs as a most important political and ideological objective.

Most of the boys and the girls who arrived from Europe after the war
were refugees who lost their families, wandered across Europe, were
persecuted, or lived in hiding, and most had no regular schooling. On
the one hand they were difficult to work with because of the traumas
they had experienced; on the other hand their educators regarded them
as ideological clay that could be molded. They were objects of political
struggles between parties, each of them trying to get a larger quota into
its educational settings. They were children belonging to the nation
(Bentwich, 1944) who could be influenced by every or any ideological
or political movement.

Experiencing Whole Community Life

Absorbing a group of youngsters influenced kibbutz community life.
In the 1930s most kibbutz members were quite young, so very few kibbutzim had indigenous youth (Landshut, 1944). "The children [of the
KYG] added a special touch to our communities. Through them the kibbutz obtained the shape of an agricultural community . . . The kibbutzim
need . . . a continuity of generations, a youth life" (Baratz, 1936, p. 2).
"[The KYG] is a way of life that can be the basis for education. No child
will grow up among us if we do not have the ability to educate youth."[6]

Thus KYG education allowed at that time a kind of simulation of a
complete, collective community life, bypassing for the time being the
need to confront its real consequences for the communal way of life.

Difference and Identity

While at the political level of discourse the youths are immediately
welcomed, at the social and cultural level they are differentiated and defined as "Others." An educator from Degania writes in 1938:

The pioneering youth who came to the country in the first waves of immigration . . . was equipped with the knowledge of Hebrew, Jewish culture, and national ideals that he sucked from his mother's breasts, that he absorbed in the *Heder* [the first Jewish schooling] and in the [Zionist] Movement. Thus he was an immediate addition of power to the Hebrew community.

The youth who arrives [now] from Western Europe is stripped of all our spiritual properties, alienated to our language and culture . . . We have here a formless matter that can be molded and given the shape we desire . . . *Only an immense mental revolution, only the destruction of all the bridges* can generate the miracle of a quick and full penetration into our problems and into the original Hebrew culture. (Pevzner, 1938, p. 86) (emphasis in the original)

The KYG residents are described as very different from the "real" pioneers who came from Eastern Europe between the beginning of the century and the beginning of the 1920s (in the second and the third waves of immigration) and established the first kibbutzim. They lack all the properties that those pioneers had. Therefore they have to be re-socialized, their past erased, and their family abandoned in order to acquire the new identity.

Nevertheless, becoming an authentic kibbutz member is not possible, because unlike previous immigrants they were driven by circumstances whereas the genuine pioneers came voluntarily, as explained by an educator in a kibbutz of the *Hashomer Hatzair* movement, who wrote in 1940:

More than 6,000 adolescents made *Aliyah* through Youth Aliyah. "Made *Aliyah?*" No. They were brought here. There is a basic difference, a decisive one. This youth lacks the unique and unforgotten experience that is flaming like a pillar of fire in the heart of each of us: This is the day of *Aliyah* [coming to the country]; a conscious, freely chosen *Aliyah*. (Shwartz, 1940)

By comparing themselves to the KYG residents kibbutz members constructed their identity as the real pioneers, as those who rebelled against their fate and made their own life decisions, leaving home and community and abandoning studies or promising career tracks to go to the unknown and to create a new and unique way of life. The presence of the KYG as a separate group at the periphery of the kibbutz community indicated to its "original" members as well as to outsiders who were the real avant-garde and nation builders. This divisive practice served in constructing the social identity of the kibbutz member.

Along with differentiating the Other one can find texts referring to some kibbutz members' inappropriate manners such as not speaking in Hebrew among themselves, coming late to work, and in a religious kibbutz not being strict enough in observing religious rules. The presence of KYG in the kibbutz is used by the community leaders to reflect back to kibbutz members their inappropriate behavior and thus as a means of social control within the community.

The discourse of the kibbutz movement leaders about the KYG as the Other, as exemplified above, elevated the kibbutz member to the level of a *Halutz* (pioneer) and a member of an elite but also subjugated him to this ideal image and made him controlled by the community and self-controlled by the ideals he formed and believed. Thus KYGs contributed to the constitution of the kibbutz subject.

The 1950s and the 1960s

Following the vast immigration of the early 1950s, the KYG population changed again. The KYGs now consisted of immigrant youth who arrived in the country with their parents, so the kibbutz ceased to be *in loco parentis*. The reasons for sending them away from home to be educated were the families' poor economic situation and the poor educational facilities in their temporary locations of residence. The rationale for offering them this kind of education was the belief that the kibbutz is a successful means of acculturation, as demonstrated in previous years.

Also, the cultural gap between the kibbutz members (including its young generation) and the KYG residents became wider: Most of the newcomers had not been members of youth movements, had no Zionist education, and–the most salient characteristic–gradually most of the KYGs consisted of youth emigrating from Moslem countries. No wonder then that a central issue of the discourse at period was the right of the kibbutz to mold them according to its ideals and concepts, especially if these were opposed to the youths' home culture. A participant in a KYG educators' convention in 1950 says:

> As a nation building its country, we have a moral and national right to separate the children from their parents. Perhaps by this we pave the road to the kibbutz for some of the parents. We sever the youth from a past we would like him to depart from, wishing to in-

tegrate him into our life. We too were cut off from our parents, and we did it willingly. We want these youths also to be severing willingly . . . He who says [settling the] Negev [desert] and blossoming wasteland must go all the way through cutting off. This is the truth, the only Zionist truth . . . and we have the right to do it for the sake of the children and the youth. We cannot leave them with their parents and let them return to their past. (Likrat Atzmeinu, 1950, pp. 14-15)

In contrast to the youths' parents, the kibbutz represents ideas such as the future, national interests, and altruism–the image of the modern subject–hence it has the right to decide on the education these immigrant youths deserve. Since the kibbutz founders rebelled against their own parents as youth, they know better than any parent what the younger generation now needs.

This patronizing approach, based on the kibbutz pioneering experience and ethos, reflected the effort to preserve the political and cultural domination it had acquired in a society that was undergoing major changes. The saying, "we want these youths also to be severing willingly" expressed the hegemonic expectation that the subordinates adopt its perspective willingly.

When Youth Aliyah leaders requested that KYG educators enable the children to keep some religious traditions like having kosher food, not eating leavened bread during Passover, or separating boys' and girls' quarters, the reaction was:

It is inconceivable that someone should come and tell us to do like this and not like that. The kibbutz movement . . . has consolidated during many years of development in *Eretz Israel* a mode of life that we are not going to cancel . . . We are a pioneering movement, we are a dynamic movement, we regard ourselves as a central factor in building Israel, and we are not going to let anyone intervene in our life by the threat of not letting us grow. (Likrat Atzmeinu, 1950, p. 13)

In the new national agenda after independence (in 1948), the kibbutz lost much of the influence it had as one of the main instruments of national goals, especially since the large immigration of the first years of independence caused a great change in the composition of the Israeli population. Many sectors of Israeli society no longer regarded the kibbutz as a model for a way of life or as an idealistic society. As indicated,

KYG students came from cultures not very favorable, or even hostile, to kibbutz ideals.

KYG members became the representatives of the Other Israel that abandoned the pioneering spirit. "Remembering the city winds blowing in the alleys of the kibbutz, spirits of liquidating national and human values, no wonder then that . . . there is not much sympathy for the KYG in the kibbutz community, especially among the second generation of kibbutz members" (Nardi, 1959, p. 270).

The attitude of kibbutz members towards KYGs became more ambivalent with a tension between the need to expand and maintain the image and position of the kibbutz in Israeli society and a desire to preserve its unique culture, assumed by kibbutz members as being threatened by the newcomers. Leaders of kibbutz movements tried hard to persuade kibbutzim to take in new KYGs. However, fewer KYGs were admitted and the number of students decreased from 4054 in 1960 to 1720 in 1970 (Gottesmann, 1971). The tendency of the kibbutz to seclude itself from certain sectors of the Israeli society became more evident (Ben-Horin, 1983; Lewenberg, 1964).

1970s and 1980s

In 1971, Youth Aliyah decided on a massive intake of disadvantaged Israeli youth into its educational programs, and the goals were changed from acculturation of immigrant adolescents to socialization of indigenous, disadvantaged youth. This change, connected with falling numbers of immigrants, reflected ideological trends toward desegregation and anxiety as to the consequences of the ethnic conflict in Israeli society (Arieli, Kashti, & Shlasky, 1983; Kashti, 1979).

Following this decision, Youth Aliyah directors made an effort to convince kibbutz leaders to increase absorption of KYGs, believing that it would contribute to social integration in education. As a result the number of KYG residents grew by several hundreds, and by the end of the 1980s all KYGs consisted of Israeli-born, disadvantaged youngsters, mostly of Oriental origin and of relatively low scholastic achievements.

Compared to previous periods, much less has been written about KYGs by kibbutz leaders during this period. Presumable this reflects a diminishing interest in the project. The text that according to my experience[7] best represents this period is an article describing KYGs in two kibbutzim, published in a special issue of the teachers' union biweekly (Nitzan, 1984) dedicated to education in the kibbutzim. The change of goals in relation to the KYGs is described as follows:

> Kibbutzim that decided positively [to take in KYGs] regarded it as a Zionist goal of educating disadvantaged Israeli youths . . . rather than making them kibbutz members. They regard the problems of disadvantaged youth as a problem of the Israeli society and feel they have to contribute. (p. 17)

The kibbutz members consider themselves accountable, in a way, for the well-being and cultural standards of the entire Israeli society; this is now what Zionism stands for. It is an altruism that might be demanded of those regarding themselves as the "serving elite" (Elon, 1981) of the Israeli society. Marda, a KYG teacher from Kibbutz *Revadim,* says:

> We regard this enterprise as Zionism. True, we are not interested in all of them to stay for good in the kibbutz, and I definitely know there are some that by no chance will be kibbutz members. However, if I manage to inculcate in them standards such as the need to strive without making calculations, the will to act and advance, to watch not only Jordan and Egypt TV but also Israeli documentary and political programs, and make them read, and if I know that they are going to function well outside–my aim is achieved . . . When they see my husband, who is the kibbutz production coordinator, cleaning the floor or girls working in the cultivation of fields, it does something to them . . . We try to show them that there are other songs besides Michael Jackson . . . When we have evenings of community singing, at first they arrive under coercion, but after a while they get used to it and perhaps something sticks. (Nitzan, 1984, p. 18)

The values to be inculcated were now almost typical modern, middle-class values and represented the urban as well as the kibbutz *Ashkenazi* (European) elite. The kibbutz was now identified with the Israeli social center and had no longer a unique and differentiated identity as a pioneering group or social avant-garde. The "lower" culture of the social sector represented by the KYG residents, as described by Marda (the teacher), was regarded as a threat to the values and culture of those who regarded themselves as the social center. By educating KYGs, the kibbutz tried to induce them to accept the hegemonic culture and thus to ensure its reproduction as well as to evoke a more favorable attitude towards the kibbutz enterprise itself. The account goes on:

> Kenny [the KYG educator] admits that there are kibbutz youths who don't like making too much effort and whose character should be improved. This is the reason why he prefers the KYG to study in a separate class, apart from the kibbutz youth. When they grumble that the kibbutz youths are allowed to go barefoot or let their hair grow long [while they are not] we tell them, "Be proud you [behave] well." The most dangerous thing is that they might lose their identity. They have to be constantly reminded why they are here. My answer is "You are here to be educated." In a concluding discussion five years later they say, "It was good for us that you kept a close rein on us." (Nitzan, 1984)

Kenny, the KYG educator, explains his methods for a successful co-optation. "First, we have to demand more of those who are to be converted than of those who belong. Second, separation is essential for the benefit of the Other, and third, they have always to be reminded that they are different than the kibbutz, native-born youth in order to preserve their identity."

Behind the veil of educational discourse other motives can be identified. The KYG members are segregated because their manners do not qualify them to live and study together with the kibbutz youth. Though not all of the latter behave well, they can on the whole be trusted and not restricted too much in their conduct, whereas the KYG members have to be watched carefully and their separate identity maintained. By signifying the different behavior and appearance of those who live near but do not belong, the separate identity and superior position of the kibbutz youth are constructed.

This paternalistic approach could not last long, because the KYG residents resented it. Youth Aliyah put pressure on kibbutzim to integrate the KYGs with the kibbutz youths–either within school or in social activities and living quarters. A few kibbutzim integrated them fully but not before selecting them very carefully. Some did it partially and some continued to segregate, but more kibbutzim stopped accepting KYGs entirely. It seems that the kibbutz movement gave up efforts to influence other cultural sectors of Israeli society and preferred keeping its position and identity through withdrawal rather than through interference. The gaps seemed to be unbridgeable.

In the early 1990s KYGs stopped accepting Israeli-born youth. Instead, the groups are composed of youth brought from the former USSR after having been selected carefully as to their academic abilities—to be educated in Israel as a first step and incentive for immigration of the whole family (Bendes-Yaakov & Friedman, 1996). The number of residents in this program in kibbutzim now is several hundreds. In a way KYGs returned to its original population: immigrant youth who come into the country without their parents. However, the political situation as well as the kibbutz and its needs are different now. It seems that national interests, based on Zionist ideals of saving young Jewish people from uncertain political situations in their native lands in the Diaspora, combine here with economic interests of the kibbutz to offer educational services in its under-occupied facilities. Likewise, the schools of the kibbutzim accept now, after a careful selection, students from the neighborhood communities in order to fill up classes and increase their students' population. The financial factor no less than the educational one plays here an important role. Further inquiry is needed to study the new situation.

CONCLUSION

Unlike many other contemporary and historical collective communities around the world and throughout history, the kibbutz did not regard itself as a secluded, esoteric sect whose desire was to limit contacts with the environment. On the contrary, since it was at its beginning one of the main instruments of the political leadership for securing Jewish domination in the country, it regarded itself as avant-garde and a main actor in the renewal of Jewish national life. The consolidation of its identity and patterns of life, as well as securing its position in the wider society, were essential in the dynamic political, economic, and demographic situation prevailing in the country. However, the possibility of becoming a secluded sect instead of a leading group and part of the elite was frightening.

One of the mechanisms used by the kibbutz to ensure continuous interaction with other sectors, to maintain its position in the wider society, and to examine constantly the boundaries of its identity was the education of KYGs. With its readiness to admit large groups of youth to live and be educated within its communities rather than letting them be put in institutions, the kibbutz undoubtedly served an important humane and national need. By this the kibbutz movement reinforced its position in Israeli society as the agent of important national missions. Of no less importance for the kibbutz was to ensure, through the absorption of youth groups, appropriate human reserves for its further development and a supportive periphery of those who did not join. In discussions and debates over questions like how to educate and who was fit to join, the kibbutz had to deal with the definition of its identity and its limits of tolerance.

The identity of the kibbutz has changed to a large extent. It moved from an image of a *Halutz,* a pioneer who devoted himself to demanding national missions of settlement and defense, to that of a socialist, nation-oriented, "serving elite" who takes part in national political and administrative causes. Later it changed to the image of a regular Israeli, upper middle-class elite. The changing KYG population in each period signified in the kibbutz community the "Other" culture that had to be denounced and rejected, thus consolidating the changing identity of the kibbutz.

The original purpose of creating the KYG was saving Jewish children and youth in need through immigration to the Jewish homeland and incorporating them in the national project of inhabiting and constructing this homeland. The means were to integrate them in the evolving communities of the kibbutzim for education and work until they were grown up enough to construct their own kibbutz. The combination of being involved in a genuine national mission with immediate integration into an evolving community of relatively young and enthusiastic people seemed an ideal formula for absorption and the forming of sound identity in a situation of traumatic change. The educational impact was impressive and many followed this path, especially those who identified completely with the enterprise and in a way submitted themselves to the model of the "genuine" kibbutz member. However, there were many that could not or did not want to follow this path and were expelled or left before finishing their period of education.[8]

After the establishment of the state of Israel, KYGs were dedicated mainly to help regular educational agencies incorporate immigrant and disadvantaged native-born youths into the Israeli society by placing them in an "educating community," thus exposing them to the ideals of the kibbutz.

This process involved separating the novices and stripping them of former identities and traits. The reasoning and legitimization used by kibbutz actors was at first overt and direct and involved the terminology of power in the definition of goals. Gradually, along with the acceptance of more pluralistic ideas in the Israeli society and the inability to keep KYG residents in complete educational seclusion (e.g., studying in separate classes and outside the kibbutz school) as in previous years, the discourse of kibbutz actors changed from a mainly political one to a more "educational" discourse: the necessity of the youths' awareness of their own need to be changed in order to join the mainstream. Nevertheless, success was only partial; youths had the option of leaving, and many did.

Discourse on education for the younger generation seems to be an important means for a community to reflect upon its identity. This discourse becomes crucial when it relates to the encounter with newcomers who are regarded as a contribution to the community but also as a threat. As shown in this study, discourse about KYGs, started by political leaders, moved during the second phase from educational leaders to professionals in education and almost disappeared in recent years. These changes exemplify the move of the kibbutz from a movement that regarded education of youth in need as taking a political part in a national and humanistic mission to a community that provides educational services to meet public needs, and, recently, to a setting offering its educational facilities mainly as a commercial service. The changes in the KYG program resembled the changes of the kibbutz identity and served it.

NOTES

1. In former years it consisted of 40-50 boys and girls. In recent years it usually consists of 20-30 residents.

2. Avnat, Rosner & Bareli, 1988; Ben-Natan & Barzily, 1982; Cohen-Raz, 1963; Galili, 1981; Gottesmann, 1971; Israel, 1985; Shalom, 1979; Wolins, 1971; Youth Aliyah, 1942.

3. Bar-Netzer, 1971; Ben-Peretz, Giladi & Dror, 1992; Kaneti-Baruch, 1961; Kohlberg, 1971; Reinhold, 1953; Seker, 1985; Snarey, 1987.

4. Horowitz, 1942; Nadad & Achiram, 1962; Shalom, 1982.

5. There were at least five different kibbutz movements at that time, each attached to a political party or movement.

6. Y. Tabenkin, in addressing the general assembly of kibbutz Givat Brener when the possibility of in taking a KYG in 1935 was discussed (Rubens, 1985, p. 9).

7. From mid 1970s until the beginning of the 1990s I was a *Youth Aliyah* supervisor to several KYGs.

8. The average rate of dropout in KYGs along the years was about 57 percent (Nadad & Achiram, 1962; Shalom, 1978; Shalom, 1982).

AUTHOR NOTE

Simha Shlasky is a Dr. (PhD), who teaches research methods in education in Derby University (the Israeli extension). His special areas of research are residential education, youth culture and the kibbutz community. Among his recent publications (in Hebrew) as an editor or co-editor and writer are "Teaching and Education: An Israeli Lexicon" (Ramot, 1987), "Community of Youth: Studies on Israeli Boarding Schools" (Ramot, 2000), and "Sexuality and Gender in Education" (Ramot, 2000).

REFERENCES

Arieli, M., Kashti, Y., & Shlasky, S. (1983). *Living at school: Israeli residential schools as people-processing organizations*. Tel Aviv: Ramot.

Avnat, A., Rosner, M., & Bareli, C. (1988). The influence of kibbutz education on second-generation immigrant youth of oriental origin. In M. Gottesmann (Ed.), *Cultural transition: The case of immigrant youth* (pp. 121-139). Jerusalem: The Magnes Press.

Baratz, Y. (1935). Ha'noar mi'germania [The youth from Germany]. *Niv Ha'kvutza*, Jan., p. 6. (in Hebrew)

Baratz, Y. (1936). Aliyat ha'noar mi'germania [Youth Aliyah from Germany]. *Niv Ha'kvutza* 15, 2. (in Hebrew)

Bar-Netzer, H. (1971). Stages in the development of youth groups and the role of the madrich. In M. Wolins, & M. Gottesmann (Eds.), *Group care: An Israeli approach* (pp. 111-123). New York: Gordon & Breach.

Bendes-Yaakov, O., & Friedman, Y. (1996). *"Naale": Noar oleh lelo horim [Immigrant youth without its parents]*. Jerusalem: Szold Institute. (in Hebrew)

Ben-Horin, Z. (1983). *Kibbutzim ve'ayarot pituach: Mi'paternalism le'shutafut [Kibbutzim and developing towns: From paternalism to cooperation]*. Haifa: Research Institute of the Kibbutz. (in Hebrew)

Ben-Natan, C., & Barzily, N. (1982). *Klitat hevrot noar bvait-ha'sefer ha'nisuii Hof-Ha'carmel [The absorption of Youth Aliyah groups in Hof Hacarmel experimental school]*. Tel Aviv: Seminar Hakibbutzim. (in Hebrew)

Ben-Peretz, M. Giladi, M., & Dror, Y. (1992). The Anne Frank Haven: A case of an alternative educational program in an integrative kibbutz setting. *International Review of Education* 38(1), 47-63.

Bentwich, N. (1944). *Jewish youth comes home: The study of Youth Aliyah 1933-1944*. London: Gollancz.

Cohen-Raz, R. (1963). *Kechol hanearim [Like all the kids: The rehabilitation of difficult youth in the kibbutz]*. Jerusalem: Youth Aliyah & Szold Institute. (in Hebrew)

Dreyfus, H.L., & Rabinow, P. (1982). *Michel Foucault: Beyond structuralism and hermeneutics*. New York: Harvester Wheatsheaf.

Elon, A. (1981). *The Israelis*. Jerusalem: Adam.

Fisk, J. (1998). Audiencing: Cultural practice and cultural studies. In N. K. Denzin & Y. S. Lincoln (Eds.), *The landscape of qualitative research: Theories and issues* (pp. 359-378). Thousand Oaks: Sage.

Foucault, M. (1972). *The archeology of knowledge*. New York: Harper.

Galili, A. (1981). *Histaglut yaldai hutz la'kibbutz [The Adjustment of "External Children" to Kibbutz Life]*. M.A. thesis. Haifa University. (in Hebrew)

Gottesmann, M. (1971). An immigrant Youth Group and its absorption in a kibbutz. In M. Wolins & M. Gottesmann (Eds.), *Group care: An Israeli approach* (pp. 90-110). New York: Gordon & Breach.

Gottesmann, M. (1987). *Aliyat ha'noar: Hemshechiut ve'shinui [Youth Aliyah: Continuity and change]*. Tel Aviv: Cherikover. (in Hebrew)

Hazan, Y. (1984). *Baiit kolet umechanech: Pirkai avar be'chinuch hevrot noar [A home of absorption and education: Chapters in the past of Youth Groups' education]*. Ramat Ha'shofet. (in Hebrew)

Horowitz, Y. (1942). *Bograi aliyat ha'noar [Youth Aliyah graduates]*. Jerusalem: Youth Aliyah. (in Hebrew)

Israel, Y. (1985). *Hevrat noar be'kibbutz ke''irgun hivrut [Kibbutz youth group as a socializing organization]*. M.A. thesis, Tel Aviv University. (in Hebrew)

Kaneti-Baruch, M. (1961). Maakav acharai hevrat noar be'kibbutz [A follow-up on a kibbutz youth group]. *Megamot 11*(2), 124-141. (in Hebrew)

Kashti, Y. (1979). *The socializing community: Disadvantaged adolescents in Israeli youth villages*. Tel Aviv: Tel Aviv University.

Kohlberg, L. (1971). Cognitive-developmental theory and the practice of collective moral education. In M. Wolins & M. Gottesmann (Eds.), *Group care: An Israeli approach* (pp. 342-379). New York: Gordon & Breach.

Landshut, S. (1944). *Hakvutza [The collective: A sociological study of the collective community in Palestine]*. Jerusalem: Hamachon Le'haskala Tzionit. (in Hebrew)

Lewenberg, A. (1964). *Pirkai Kiryat Shmona [Chapters from Kiryat Shmona]*. Tel Aviv: Schocken. (in Hebrew)

Likrat Atzmeinu (toward ourselves), (1950). A protocol of KYG Educators Conference in the Kibbutz Ha'rtzi, March 1950. Youth Aliyah Documentation Center, File 623.1 (12). (in Hebrew)

Levant, Z. (1940). Ha'noar ha'oleh ba'kibbutz ha'artzi [The immigrant youth in the Kibbutz Ha'rtzi.] In *Im ha'noar ha''oleh [Being with the Immigrant Youth]* (p. 11). Merchavia: Hakibutz Ha'rtzi. (in Hebrew)

Nadad, A., & Achiram, E. (1962). *Chanichai aliyat ha'noar be'haiim atzmaiim [Youth Aliyah graduates in independent life.]* Jerusalem: Youth Aliyah. (in Hebrew)

Nardi, S. (1959). Mifal aliyat ha'noar [Youth Aliyah enterprise]. *Niv Hakvutza 8*, 2 (30), 270. (in Hebrew)

Nitzan, A. (1984). Anaf hevrat ha'noar [The Youth Group Sector]. *Hed Hachinuch 59* (3), 16-19. (in Hebrew)

Pevzner, D. (1938). Tipulenu ba'noar ha'oleh [Our care taking of the immigrant youth]. *Niv ha'kvutza 19*, 86-88. (in Hebrew)

Potter, J. (1997). Discourse analysis as a way of analyzing naturally occurring talk. In D. Silverman (Ed.), *Qualitative research: Theory, method and practice* (pp. 144-160). Thousand Oaks: Sage.

Reinhold, C. (1953). *Noar boneh baito: Aliyat ha'noar ke''tnua chinuchit [Youth builds its home: Youth Aliyah as an educational movement]*. Tel Aviv: Am Oved. (in Hebrew)

Rubens, A. (Ed.). (1985). *Yovel hevrat ha'noar A (1935-1985)* [*The jubilee of the first youth group (1935-1985)*]. Givat Brener. (in Hebrew)

Seker, Z. (1985). *Baiit sheni ba'kibbutz* [*A second home in the kibbutz*]. Tel Aviv: Sifriat Poalim. (in Hebrew)

Shalom, H. (1978). *Azivat chanichim et mi'misgarot aliyat ha''noar* [*Students'dropout of Youth Aliyah frameworks*]. Jerusalem: Youth Aliyah. (in Hebrew)

Shalom, H. (1979). The youth group and the kibbutz. *Youth Aliyah Bulletin*, Aug., 18-25.

Shalom, H. (1982). *Chanichai aliyat hanoar ba'kibbutzim: Mechkar maakav acharai bogrim* [*Youth Aliyah students in kibbutzim: Follow-up study of graduates*]. Jerusalem: Youth Aliyah. (in Hebrew)

Shwartz, A. (1940). *Im hanoar ha'oleh* [*Being with the immigrant youth*] (pp. 15-18). Merchavia: Hakibutz Ha'hartzi. (in Hebrew)

Snarey, J. (1987). Promoting moral maturity among adolescents: An ethnographic study of the Israeli kibbutz. *Comparative Educational Review 31*(2), 241-259.

Tabenkin, Y. (1942). Beit ha'sefer ve'hamilchama [The school and the war]. *Tzror Michtavim Le'shelot Ha'chinuch Ha'mshutaf 7*, 1-15. (in Hebrew)

Tzizling, A. (1939). Yishuvim mechanchim [Educating communities]. *Tzror Michtavim 59*(124), 1-7. (in Hebrew)

Umansky, D. (1939). Aliyat ha'noar be'hever ha'kvutzot [Youth Aliyah in Hever Hkvutzot]. *Niv Hakvutza 20*, 69-74. (in Hebrew)

Wolins, M. (1971). The kibbutz as a foster mother: Maimonides applied. In M. Wolins & M. Gottesmann (Eds.), *Group care: An Israeli approach* (pp. 73-89). New York: Gordon & Breach.

Youth Aliyah. (1942). *Me'hayir la'kfar* [*From the town to the village*]. Jerusalem: Youth Aliyah. (in Hebrew)

Social and Academic Integration
of City and Kibbutz Youth

Edna Shoham

SUMMARY. The article describes two kibbutz secondary schools that have absorbed city children and seeks to examine whether and to what extent kibbutz educational perceptions reflect integration between kibbutz and city children. In both schools absorption and integration are central educational themes. This policy is expressed in arrangements in both schools and kibbutz that stress social and academic integration of the city children with their kibbutz peers. Components of collective education, which emphasize values, cooperation, and education for a life of work contribute much to the encounter with city children. This group is exposed to varied venues of social and work activities, and this advances the process of integration into the absorbing society. However, the situation is different with regard to individualistic components in the educational policy that nurture individual achievements. These obstruct integration, because those doing the absorbing fear that academic progress will suffer as a result of taking in students from weaker population strata. *[Article copies available for a fee from The Haworth Document Delivery Service: 1-800-342-9678. E-mail address: <getinfo@ haworthpressinc.com> Website: <http://www. HaworthPress.com> © 2001 by The Haworth Press, Inc. All rights reserved.]*

KEYWORDS. Youth Aliyah, educational integration, urban youth, kibbutz youth, kibbutz education, collective education, youth services

---

Edna Shoham is affiliated with Oranim and Haifa University.

[Haworth co-indexing entry note]: "Social and Academic Integration of City and Kibbutz Youth." Shoham, Edna. Co-published simultaneously in *Child & Youth Services* (The Haworth Press, Inc.) Vol. 22, No. 1/2, 2001, pp. 75-92; and: *Innovative Approaches in Working with Children and Youth: New Lessons from the Kibbutz* (ed: Yuval Dror) The Haworth Press, Inc., 2001, pp. 75-92. Single or multiple copies of this article are available for a fee from The Haworth Document Delivery Service [1-800-342-9678, 9:00 a.m. - 5:00 p.m. (EST). E-mail address: getinfo@haworthpressinc.com].

75

Many studies have examined the characteristics of Israel's residential school education and its effects on students (Arieli, 1992; Kashti & Arieli, 1976). Residential schools are effective in developing social skills as well as positive attitudes about education (Kashti & Arieli, 1976; Smilensky & Nevo, 1970). The effectiveness of residential schools is attributed mainly to structural and organizational factors and to psychological changes in the student (Kashti & Sagi, 1992), the result of changed surroundings:

1. Removal from a depriving background and intensive exposure to an inclusive institution that preempts conflicts between family and community of origin on the one hand, and school on the other, helping the student acquire the norms of the cultural mainstream.
2. The residential school helps the student who experienced failure and frustration in day school to turn over a new leaf. Students are rewarded for a variety of behaviors and have new opportunities for success.
3. Peer group influence is positive. The intensive interaction between residential school students makes their peers, who are the immediate and primary frame of reference, into a powerful and influential group.

Eisikovitz and Beck (1992) describe two different perceptions about what absorption should mean. One maintains that absorption means complete assimilation while in the other view absorption means integration–combining with the new culture. The former is anchored in the ideology of Zionism as a melting pot in which all sectors of the Israeli population must give up their uniqueness and adopt the culture of the dominant group. The latter sees Israeli society as a multicultural one that must participate in the burden of adaptation carried by minority groups.

Sever (1997) uses four parameters to distinguish the ways in which successful educational institutions deal with the absorption task: (a) The school staff seeks to combine the culture of the newcomers with the absorbing culture; (b) the absorption task is a high priority of the school; (c) students being integrated have an effect on the school climate and culture; and (d) school activities are marked by initiative and adaptation.

In the kibbutz educational system much emphasis is placed on a willingness to be involved, on one's social contribution, and adopting an active stance (Frank, 1993). These find expression in absorbing youth in distress and immigrant youth in the kibbutzim. The familiar model is the integration of children and adolescents in the youth societies of the kibbutz. The youth society in this context is a residential framework designed for youths coming to the kibbutz from different places in Israel. Its members live in the kibbutz, informally adopted by families there, and are part of the kibbutz school.

There are three main forms of integration: (a) An independent youth society that does not become part of the youth society of the kibbutz, its members studying in a separate class at the district school; (b) an independent youth society that exists as a separate framework, but its members study in regular classes of the district school with kibbutz children; or (c) the youth society is fully integrated socially and academically–living, learning, and working with the kibbutz children (Arieli, 1980; Israel, 1985; Seker, 1984). The second model, where integration between the outside youth society and that of the kibbutz is not complete, is the most common. Integration conditions are more complex in the kibbutz than elsewhere (Seker, 1984), because youth groups from the weakest strata of Israeli society encounter others from among the strongest socio-economically, and the encounter takes place in the territory of the stronger group.

Several studies describe the way city youth are absorbed in the kibbutz including adaptation problems, the educational stages in the development of youth societies, and characteristic interpersonal dynamics and relationships of the education process (Alon, 1981; Altman, 1984; Avnat, 1988; Bar-Netzer, 1970; Galili, 1981; Israel, 1985; Seker, 1984; Wallins, 1970). In this article we discuss absorption patterns in one kibbutz movement, *Hakibbutz Ha'rtzi*,[1] because of its special educational focus expressed in the way it runs the 17 institutions for students in Grades 7 through 12. The typical institution is a residential school usually belonging to four or five neighboring kibbutzim. It is a social and educational unit that embraces all aspects of students' lives and emphasizes granting full autonomy to the youth society. Lavi (1990) differentiates *Hakibbutz Ha'rtzi* institutions from other kibbutz schools by their endeavors to include most aspects of its students' lives and by how adult counselors are intensively involved in the independent youth society. Because of its range of academic, work, and social activities, students can establish their social status outside the limitations of academic achievement.

We shall now focus on the form of absorption described as the ideal (Seker, 1984). Here the city youth society is integrated socially and academically with that of the kibbutz. This is practiced in the two educational institutions we discuss: Anne Frank Haven and Gan Shmuel. Anne Frank Haven is the district school of three kibbutzim. It was established within one kibbutz and later the other two joined. It is in the foothills of Mount Meron near the Lebanese border. Gan Shmuel belongs to only one kibbutz, bordered by it on one side and by the orchards and greenhouses that serve as laboratories on the other sides. Each school has classrooms, laboratories, a teachers' room, an auditorium, and a fine, up-to-date library belonging to both school and kibbutz.

This article is based on data from three studies: those of Nahshon Ben-David (1987), Lieberman and Dror (1995), and Ben-Peretz, Giladi, and Dror (1992), all of which are case studies of the two educational institutions.

Our analyses focus on (a) educational policy and school and kibbutz arrangements, and (b) the encounter between city and kibbutz youth, as manifested in student and staff perceptions in the social and educational world of the school.

KIBBUTZ ARRANGEMENTS IN THE ABSORPTION PROCESS AND SCHOOL EDUCATIONAL POLICY

The educational policy of both schools follows the principles of kibbutz education: (a) a combination of and balance between nurturing the learner as an individual while educating him or her as a member of a socially-aware community; (b) teacher autonomy evidenced in teachers' direct involvement in curriculum development and open and flexible attitude to the individual needs of the learners; (c) the non-selective nature of the school, which is open to the entire heterogeneous kibbutz youth population; (d) an integrative teaching approach with interconnections between various field of study; (e) the kibbutz community as an educational environment; and (f) the integration of curricula into the web of kibbutz life (Shoham, 1991). Sirgiovani (1994) states that school policy is expressed in an educational program that guides principals' and teachers' activities and decision making–daily and over long periods. While it weaves the web of school activity, this program also helps identify considerations that lay behind its goals. Every school decision should reflect commitment to its educational ideology.

Absorption (read integration) is strongly emphasized in the educational programs of both schools. This shows how important absorption is in the educational outlook of those who created the program. Thus in the program of the Anne Frank Haven, the essence of the special educational system is cooperative education and study in the residential school for kibbutz and city children alike, in groups where half the children come from the kibbutz and half from the city via Youth Aliyah (Ben-David, 1987). The educational program of Gan Shmuel is similar. Absorption is the task and the challenge that characterize the school and determine its ethos. Absorption is the distinguishing and meaningful feature of our educational outlook, and we allot many resources to them such as educational and teaching staff, adoptive kibbutz families, and special tutoring (Lieberman & Dror, 1995).

In both schools, educational staff outlines three central goals for the school absorption policy:

1. Fostering Zionist and national goals of absorbing youths from distressed strata of the population.
2. Giving kibbutz children a chance to be educated in their home kibbutz. Enlarging the school makes it possible to maintain it locally.
3. Increasing the number of kibbutz members by absorbing graduates of the school.

The definition of educational goals is determined by the educational outlook that prides itself on non-selectivity, social involvement, personal autonomy, and the democratic social experience. But there are difficulties to contend with from day to day: location, a lack of financial resources, limitations on the academic solutions available for a small group of students, and the will to maintain a local educational framework that meets the needs of the kibbutz community (Avnat, 1982; Galili, 1981; Seker, 1984).

The ideological values in both schools, which sees absorption and integration as key educational elements, finds concrete expression in arrangements to this end in school and kibbutz.

ABSORPTION ARRANGEMENTS IN SCHOOL

Structure and Organization

In grade 7, when the children transfer from local elementary schools to the educational institution of the kibbutz movement, there is a policy of taking in a group of city children. For the most part these come from disadvantaged population strata and, in recent years, waves of immigration brought in groups of youth from the former Soviet Union.

At the Anne Frank Haven, each member kibbutz that has a grade 7 class takes in a group of 16 to 24 boys and girls of that age from the city. During their first year–the absorption year–they study in a separate class and live in a separate group in the residence. The educators see three main purposes in this: an educational group coalesces, learning gaps are bridged, and kibbutz life becomes familiar. All these goals require effort. Hence each absorption group has its own staff comprised of a teacher, a housemother, and a counselor, with a view to meeting students' needs during the absorption year. As one teacher said: "The children go through a social and cultural 'boom' (like a supersonic boom) when they get to the kibbutz. It's important to give them the right habits and raise them to an acceptable level in their studies so that they can be integrated under conditions that are fair to them." In this first year the city children integrate gradually with their kibbutz peers through joint activities, the most important of which is the Bar Mitzvah program during the year of absorption, because this is when they turn 13 years old.

In grade 8 the two groups living in the residence of the same kibbutz come together in a single class. This is both an academic and a social unit, and it remains intact until the end of grade 12. In grade 8, much emphasis is placed on the integration of the two groups into one–socially and academically.

At Gan Shmuel, where just one kibbutz is involved, the system is somewhat different. Each year enough city children are taken in to fill up grade 7. Hence the number varies from year to year depending on the number of kibbutz children. There may be only a few city children some years, while in other years there are large groups and even a whole grade 7 class that may come in without a parallel class in the kibbutz. In this case the outside children have a separate homeroom class until they finish grade 12. However, numbers are generally about equal in both groups, the idea being to have two parallel classes in which integration takes place as soon as the outside group arrives. The desire to keep the residential group small enough to be intimate–about 200 children in Grades 7 to 12–restricts admissions.

Admissions

Both schools hold examinations to ascertain the students' achievement level, and they also interview the youths arriving from distressed areas. If these latter candidates' achievements are far below the national norm, they are not accepted; the assumption is that if the gap between the newcomers and the other students is too great, their absorption within the integrative framework will be very difficult, and the educational staff will be faced with problems with which they have not been trained to cope. The school's decision also takes into account the report from their previous school and the results of psychometric examinations. It is worth mentioning that identifying students from the depressed populations with a relatively high potential and fostering their advancement is one of the recommendations of the team for the advancement of distressed populations set up by the Ministry of Education (Levi, 1999).

Program Structure

In both schools incoming students become part of the three existing frameworks: heterogeneous homeroom classes in which they study history, literature, geography, and Bible, for example; homogeneous classes in subjects that are necessarily taught at different skill levels such as English, Hebrew language, and mathematics, and a variety of elective courses. All students prepare for matriculation at the end of grade 12 (Dror, 1988; Shoham, 1991), and all who are capable of doing so sit for the examinations.

This program is maintained throughout, and matriculation candidates are not separated from the other students. Teachers see matriculation as an important integrative tool that stimulates youngsters to learn, a common goal that unites the two groups.

ABSORPTION ARRANGEMENTS IN THE KIBBUTZ

A complementary facet of the school arrangements are those of the kibbutz community. Research stresses that the kibbutz is an educational community that assists integration. The kibbutz residential school is part of a community of values in which not only those directly involved in education but the whole environment has an educational role. The entire kibbutz is an educational institution: The kibbutz way of life, including weekday and holiday leisure activities, role models in the adoptive family and at work, work as a value, cooperative relationships with a sense of belonging that entails obligations to others, the democratic process, humanistic values, and a value-oriented world (Avnet, 1982; Kahane, 1991; Seker, 1984; Shalom, 1982).

Work

Work is an important and central component in the life of both the integrating and the integrated groups of children. Most show a responsible attitude about work, given the importance that society attaches to it. Students experience adult work in the service occupations, in farming, and in industry, working several hours a day after school and during vacations without compensation. In this way they come into direct contact with kibbutz members who become their role models in attitudes to work.

Social Activities

These take place in the afternoon and evening hours during the school term and during vacations. Included are committee membership, sports, hobbies, excursions, holiday observances, parties, and the school newspaper. Organization is on the basis of the same-age educational groups (school classes) and of the school as a whole.

Residence

Each kibbutz has a residence that serves all the students from the kibbutz and from the city. Age groups live in separate buildings, two or three to a room. The absorption pattern in both schools has the grade 7 children from the kibbutz and city living in different buildings, the groups uniting during the subsequent summer vacation or at the beginning of grade 8. All live in the same house with roommates from the other group and become an academic and social unit that will function until the end of grade 12.

Adoptive Families

The absorption model in both kibbutzim assigns each city student to an adoptive or foster family. Some families take in several children. The fact that some of these were themselves once foster children is a help. The foster family is a substitute of sorts for the parental home the student misses and is an additional link (besides the counselor and the housemother) between the student and the kibbutz. The youngsters generally spend an hour or two with their foster parents in the afternoon. In what way and to what extent these parents become involved with their foster children depends on what they find suitable.

Ties with Students' Parents

In the past neither school gave sufficient attention to the link with parents outside the kibbutz. The attitude was that it is better to cut the youngster off from his or her parents, since the home is in most instances a source of problems and frustrations. Now efforts are made to maintain continuous contact with the parents. The student visits them every third weekend, and the educational staff visits each family at least once a year. There are organized parental visits, and parents are kept informed about their child's school and social life, including the problems and difficulties.

CHANGES IN THE SCHOOLS

The most conspicuous change was opening kibbutz schools to day students from the moshavim and other neighboring communities. At the Anne Frank Haven in the 1994-95 school year, about 100 of the 332 students were day students. In 1990-1991 at Gan Shmuel, only 45% came from the kibbutz; the others were either residential students from city youth groups or day students. Both schools have recently begun to accept immigrant youth from the former Soviet Union whose academic and social level is closer to that of the kibbutz children.

There is an ongoing debate at the schools as to their future. Should they remain small and intimate–and unable to offer varied study options–or should they take in more students and forego intimacy? At the Anne Frank Haven there were other changes. The Gulf War in 1991 hastened the transition from kibbutz children sleeping together in their children's houses to sleeping with their families, which meant that the school class was no longer an all-embracing social group. Classes became heterogeneous with students from the three kibbutzim and those from the city in each.

ELEMENTS OF COLLECTIVE EDUCATION IN THE ABSORPTION PROCESS

Zionist-National-Kibbutz Values

Both schools are committed to these and stress the kibbutz values of equality and cooperation as central elements in their written programs.

Interviews and observations indicated that Zionist and national values found expression in teaching about Jewish holidays and in commemorating events connected with Jewish history and culture. In addition, there were informal activities such as excursions, interest and hobby groups, and discussions. A Gan Shmuel housemother talks about an excursion her group took: "This is how students become attached to the country. We talk about what we see, about the scenery, the flowers. They start picking flowers, but in this country there are protected flowers you can't pick, and this is the way to explain to them that we don't pick flowers, because they're part of the scenery of Israel."

Both city and kibbutz children encounter kibbutz values in daily living as they meet kibbutz members at work and in their social life. The value message is transmitted through a life-style observed in the kibbutz rather than through formal teaching and learning. One kibbutz youngster from Gan Shmuel says: "I'm sure the principal has educational intentions all the time; he wants us to be socialists. . . . Not much of that rubs off on us, because there's nothing real about it at school. But in the broad picture, whoever lives in the residence 24 hours a day gets some education for group living . . . living the way you do there . . . from the people and the ideas you meet . . ."

Educators stress kibbutz values of equality, cooperation, and mutual help. One who works with immigrants from the former Soviet Union said: "At first they'd see me pick up a tray and nobody even thought of helping. Today they just see me or someone else, and they come to help right away . . . We work very intensively on getting along together and helping one another."

The immigrant students appear to get this message. For example, one of them says: "In another boarding school they don't say a word to each other; they pay no attention to each other. Here everyone helps. If you ask for help, you get it." Or, "If you're sick . . . they bring your homework . . . Everyone comes and asks how you feel . . . and if there's some way to help. The kibbutz ideology is that there isn't someone low down and someone else high up, but that everyone is equal."

We see then that in both kibbutz institutions national and kibbutz values are important components of school culture and in the encounter between the students being integrated and those who integrate them. However, there appears to be insufficient attention to the culture and values of the first group who have to give up their special attributes and adopt the kibbutz culture (Eisikovitz & Beck, 1991; Sever, 1997). A housemother at Gan Shmuel mentioned with satisfaction that her group had undergone a socialization process in which the identification model was the kibbutz youth. The incoming students consciously adopted the life-style, the dress, the behavior, and the culture of kibbutz society. According to her, this integration took place with the help of two complementary models: Their own group functioned as supportive peers, and there was a supportive environment comprised of the foster family, teachers and other students.

The Social Encounter and the Absorption Process

Both groups of students and their teachers see the social encounter as successful and valuable. Teachers feel that the very meeting between kibbutz children and those with a different culture and different approaches, whom they otherwise would not have known, leads to tolerance for others who are different. Educators say that the kibbutz children are more open and more sensitive to nationwide social issues than are other kibbutz members, because they know city children.

Moreover, kibbutz children at the Anne Frank Haven grow up knowing that after grade 7, city children will join them. This they regard as quite natural. Anticipation builds up during the year, the event itself is celebrated and their emotions run high. They see the city children as their equals in rights and duties and find no significance whatever in the fact that they are from the kibbutz while those they are absorbing come from the city. "We know different people so that makes us more open-minded." The city group, too, feels they are treated as equals and sense no discrimination. They mention that they come in young and in a few years it is hard to distinguish them from the kibbutz children. A group of city children interviewed at Gan Shmuel stressed the support they received from their kibbutz peers.

> There is a togetherness, there's a social framework, and everyone has friends around him. This helps a person over difficulties and gives a lot of individual support . . . I want to say that what's special at the kibbutz is that you live with friends 24 hours a day . . . In town, if someone has a problem, he's alone. Here, from the moment we're together, everything is taken care of . . . Everyone wants to be with the others because everyone has the same problem.

The social encounter is based on mutuality with contributions from both sides. This leads to the sense of partnership and equality between the city children and their kibbutz peers, as the following shows: "I think that socially we're very active, much more than the average here at school. I think if we weren't here the institution would look different . . . I don't think any of the kibbutzniks could do what we do. We're entitled to something from the institution because we really do contribute . . . " Or, "The little ones, the lowest grade, that is, are proud of us, in my opinion, but it doesn't interest the seniors all that much. They couldn't do anything like we do and they're jealous."

Despite the sense of a positive encounter in which all sides give and receive, both schools disclose problems. At the Anne Frank Haven the social and educational work with the kibbutz seventh graders is insufficient, not preparing them adequately to absorb the city children. Educators state that they should be prepared just like the newcomers. They too should have a special staff from the kibbutz–a teacher, a housemother and a counselor–with meetings carefully planned and more cooperation between the staffs serving the two groups.

Moreover, the main effort at the Haven focuses on grade 7, after which the enlarged staff is replaced by a smaller one, adversely affecting absorption. Social activity too is inadequate after the absorption year, mainly for want of suitable counselors. The staff that works with these youth is small, so they are under pressure day after day, which leads to fatigue and burnout.

According to some students who are absorbed, although there are good relationships between kibbutz and city children, "The spark (of awareness) that he's a kibbutznik and I'm from the city can become a weapon to start something . . . Kibbutz children think too much of themselves, create a lot of tension" (Anne Frank Haven). And, "The place belongs to the kibbutz children. It's their home and not ours . . . The main thing is that *they* receive *us;* it's their home and they go home whenever they please . . . " Or, "It's not exactly discrimination, but a difference. I think it's justified. Naturally, it's their home and no end of things are easier for them because their parents are here" (Gan Shmuel).

Work and Absorption

As previously stated, work is perceived to be as important as studies and social life. It permits students to achieve distinction that does not depend on formal knowledge, and is the meeting place of kibbutz youth. The work place is not merely an economic unit but a most important social unit–a source of support and encouragement. Students from the city at Anne Frank Haven report that they know all the kibbutz members and take part in holiday celebrations and special work projects. In the senior grades they are integrated into branches of the kibbutz economy, feel attached to those who work there, and have a sense of commitment and responsibility to the places where they work.

At Gan Shmuel, according to the group being absorbed, their branch managers would support and help them if they ran into trouble at school or socially and would not let them be put out of the kibbutz. "Let's say I did something wrong socially, I think my branch manager would support me and not let me be expelled." Excellence, responsibility, and devotion at work earn social esteem for the student, sometimes more than academic performance does. The Gan Shmuel principal illustrated: "When students are assigned to pick citrus, the fastest picker is rated very high by the students." He added that work is a most important facet of the integration process.

Some students report difficulties in getting used to work but add that they develop good relations with the people they work with and who are interesting to talk to. "I work in the kindergarten between 1:30 and 4:00 in the afternoon, and that's inconvenient; it was even hard. There was no time to be at home and no time for a rest. But the people at work were fine. You could make contact with them and they're very nice." Or the student working at the duck pond: "I found it interesting . . . the work and the people too . . . I felt good there." And also, "I work in the dining room. I don't like the work but I like the people . . . It's interesting to talk to them."

THE INDIVIDUAL EDUCATIONAL ELEMENT: STUDIES AS PART OF THE ABSORPTION PROCESS

Both schools promote academic achievement and passing the matriculation examinations with flying colors. The schools' educational programs, with their Zionist and national values, inform the absorption process. Emphasis is placed on absorbing city youth so as to have more students and thus make it possible to keep the school within the kibbutz. At the same time, educators maintain that taking in a relative large number of outside children with low scholastic achievement is not good, because it affects the kibbutz children's achievements adversely. At Gan Shmuel: "On the one hand we try for high matriculation results, but on the other hand we take in city children whose learning level is low. This absorption policy is bad for the academic level of our school, and that's a problem for our students and their parents . . . People feel that heterogeneity brings down the achievements of good students." A homeroom teacher in grade 12 at Anne Frank Haven, for example, proposes scholastically homogeneous classes from grade 10. In his opinion, this will not impair social interaction, which is already well established. Among kibbutz students, too, in both schools, we heard the view that absorption works against individual academic achievements: "Because of absorbing city children, the level is going down, so we shouldn't go on doing it."

Another aspect involves teaching methods adapted to a heterogeneous school population. Teachers say that not enough use has been made of varied teaching methods that would suit the heterogeneous classes that the absorption process creates. The homeroom teacher of Grade 12 at Anne Frank Haven says: "The class of 17 could be divided into five or six levels, but no teacher is willing to use individual or group methods, which you need in a heterogeneous class . . . They're all for the expository mode that seems to promise faster achievement."

Educators say that kibbutz students are getting the message that scholastic excellence and matriculation success are the most important elements for their future. Hence they see that the students being absorbed from weak populations with a learning level below that of the kibbutz are interfering with their own progress.

Staff of both schools are aware of the problem. However, they do not succeed in using their advantages of a supportive school policy, small classes, large staffs, and a clear educational philosophy to develop the varied teaching methods that would answer the needs of the two student populations and contribute to their academic integration.

Despite the widespread view that the achievements of the kibbutz children have suffered due to the absorption project, it is emphasized by the city children that their academic achievements have improved. They cite the benefits of a school framework that makes clear demands and insists on matriculation while helping those having difficulties, encouraging them, and pulling them upward. As one such student said: "If we weren't in the kibbutz we wouldn't be in school at all. Almost all our friends in town quit in grade 11 and go to work."

The city children also declare that the egalitarian, non-formal relationship between them and the educational staff motivates them to academic achievement. Most of those we interviewed mentioned a good, supportive relationship with the staff in contrast to the cold indifference they met in previous schools. Here is how three students put it: "We all feel free to go to the teacher or the housemother any time we want, even in the afternoon and evening" (Anne Frank Haven). And, "The best thing that happened to me at school is that if I have a problem with my lessons, they understand and meet me half way." Or, "I have trouble with school work. In town they tried to help with tutorials, but the teacher didn't try to help me. I'd stop studying and start roaming around. The kibbutz helps me not only with my lessons. They lay out a way of life for us here . . . " (Gan Shmuel).

They appreciate the social framework that may serve as an alternative to that of the school. Even when one stops studying full-time, one is not a dropout and loses no social status: "At the moment I've given up part of the school program. There's nothing like this anywhere else. I'm still part of the school framework, and I still have my work. It's a great help to me. Instead of failing in all kinds of subjects, they give me a chance to study another way. That doesn't happen everywhere."

There is much evidence that graduates are satisfied with their kibbutz education (Avnet, 1982; Ben-Peretz, Giladi and Dror, 1988; Shalom, 1982). They consider the kibbutz a factor that helped them advance in their military service, motivated them to study, educated them to good citizenship, and made them more mobile socially.

The principal of Gan Shmuel bears this out: "Equality here is equal opportunity, enabling all students to develop as far as they can–not equal scholastic ability but equality of different areas. Where the only area of achievement is the intellectual one, then someone who's strong intellectually will succeed and one who is weak will fail . . . But if you give students other areas where they can express themselves, you let them win social esteem socially and esteem at work."

CONCLUSION

We sought to examine the connection between educational policy and arrangements for absorption in school and kibbutz, on the one hand, and the encounter between kibbutz youth, the absorbing group, and the city group absorbed by them on the other. The policy in both schools gives absorption and integration a central place in the educational endeavor. The definition of absorption goals is taken from the educational outlook of the school, which is egalitarian, non-selective, and socially involved. At the same time, the school faces routine difficulties such as location, insufficient resources, and size limitations, desiring as it does to have the school remain a local framework.

The centrality of absorption in school culture is manifest in school and kibbutz arrangements that emphasize the integration of studies, society, and work in their absorption system. In both schools there is an "ideal" absorption pattern (Seker, 1984) in which incoming city students are fully integrated academically and socially in the kibbutz youth society after grade 7, which was the point of transition from the local school to the regional educational institution.

In both schools the collective educational elements which stress values, cooperation, and education for social living and for work appear in the school program and in actual arrangements in the school and the kibbutz. These contribute much to the actual encounter between the two groups of children.

In contrast, individualistic elements in the educational policy that nurture high level individual achievements obstruct the absorption process and integration: Those doing the absorbing fear that academic progress will suffer as a result of taking in students from weaker population strata.

In conclusion, the integration encounter between city and kibbutz youth succeeds when there is mutuality and contributions come from both sides, that is, in the social and work areas with a view to creating a single society. Without mutuality and a basis of equality, integration suffers. Nonetheless, exposing the incoming groups to different and varied circles of experience, in at least some of which full integration is possible, is greatly to the credit of kibbutz education.

NOTE

1. In Israel there were, between 1979-2000, three kibbutz movements: The United Kibbutz Movement (Hebrew acronym *Takam*), the National Kibbutz movement (*Ha'kibbutz Ha'rtzi*) and the Religious Kibbutz movement.

AUTHOR NOTE

Edna Shoham is Dr. (PhD), Senior Teacher of Education, in the University of Haifa and Oranim. Her specializations are history teaching, teacher education and curriculum studies. She is a member of kibbutz Yifat.

REFERENCES

Alon, M. (1981). The adoptive family and absorption in the kibbutz. *Hahinuch Hameshutaf, 102*, 115-120. (in Hebrew)
Altman, H. (1984). *How kibbutz and (city) youth society children live together, life in an integrative society.* Master's thesis submitted to the School of Education, University of Tel Aviv. (in Hebrew)

Arieli, M. (1980). *Nurturing distressed youth and residential education.* Tel-Aviv: Zirkover. (in Hebrew)

Arieli, M. (Ed.). (1992). *Residential schools, their staffs and communities.* Tel-Aviv: University of Tel-Aviv. (in Hebrew)

Avnet, A. (1982). *The effect of youth society education on youth from oriental communities.* Haifa: University of Haifa, Kibbutz Education Research Institute. (in Hebrew)

Avnet, A. (1988). The kibbutz youth society as an intercultural encounter. *Hakibbutz, 12,* 177-194. (in Hebrew)

Ben-David, N. (1987). *The Anne Frank Haven as an integration model.* Bet Berl College. (in Hebrew)

Bar-Netzer, H. (1970, Spring). The kibbutz as a foster mother. *Alim, l'Inyanei Hinuch b'Aliyat Hanoar,* Spring, 27-36. (in Hebrew)

Ben-Peretz, M., Giladi, M., & Dror, Y. (1992). The Anne Frank Haven: An educational program in an integrative kibbutz setting. *International Review of Education, 38,* 47-63.

Dror, Y. (1988). Kibbutz education ideology applied at the secondary level. *Hahinuch Hameshutaf, 128,* 45-63. (in Hebrew)

Eisikovitz, R., & Beck, R. (1991). Models for the education of immigrant children in Israel. *Iyunim b'Hinuch, 52,* 33-50. (in Hebrew)

Frank, A. (1993). Whither the educational institution? *Hahinuch Hameshutaf, 148-149,* 34-37. (in Hebrew)

Galili, A. (1981). *Adaptation of outside children to the kibbutz.* Graduation thesis submitted to the University of Haifa. (in Hebrew)

Israel, Y. (1985). *The youth society as a socialization agent: Processes and events in adaptation.* Master's thesis submitted to the University of Haifa. (in Hebrew)

Kahane, R. (1991). Structure of the socialization process and its effect on adaptation patterns. *Iyunim b'Hinuch, 55/56,* 51-66. (in Hebrew)

Kashti, Y., & Sagi, Y. (1992). Social encounters in a comprehensive residential school. In M. Arieli (Ed.), *Residential schools, their staffs and communities.* Tel-Aviv: University of Tel Aviv School of Education, Socialization and Community Education Unit. (in Hebrew)

Kashti, Y., & Arieli, M. (Eds.). (1976). *Residential schools: Socialization processes in an active environment.* Tel-Aviv: Daga. (in Hebrew)

Lavi, Z. (1990). Is the educational institution still necessary? *Hahinuch Hameshutaf, 138,* 1-9. (in Hebrew)

Levi, A. (1999). The advancement of students from distressed populations. In A. Peled (Ed.), *Fifty Years of the Israeli Educational System* (109-135), (vol.1).

Lieberman, Y., & Dror, Y. (1995). *Four schools, four worlds.* Oranim: Kibbutz Education Research Institute. (in Hebrew)

Seker, Z. (1984). *Integration with kibbutz children.* Jerusalem: The Jewish Agency, Youth Aliyah, Education and Guidance Division. (in Hebrew)

Sever, R. (1997). *The intercultural bridge in Israel-why we need it and how to build it.* Yeshut, a Project for Absorbing Immigrant Students in the Educational System, Jerusalem: Institute for Research on Nurturing Education, School of Education of the Hebrew University in Jerusalem. (in Hebrew)

Shalom, H. (1982). *Youth Aliyah in the kibbutz.* Jerusalem: Youth Aliyah. (in Hebrew)

Shoham, E. (1991). Autonomous curricula in the kibbutz secondary school and their link with kibbutz educational ideology. Ph.D. thesis submitted to the University of Tel Aviv. (in Hebrew)

Sirgiovani, T. J. (1994). *Building community in schools.* San Francisco: Jossey-Bass.

Smilansky, M., & Nevo, D. (1970). *Gifted graduates of the residential school project from disadvantaged social strata.* Tel-Aviv & Jerusalem: University of Tel Aviv and Szold Institute. (in Hebrew)

Wallins, M. (1970, Spring). The kibbutz as a foster mother. *Alim, l'Inyanei Hinuch b'Aliyat Hanoar*, 14-27. (in Hebrew)

One Russian "Chevrat Noar" Group in the Kibbutz: An Assessment of the Na'aleh Program

Orit Bendas-Jacob

SUMMARY. Since 1992, the Na'aleh program has been bringing youth from the Confederation of Independent States (CIS) to study in Israel without their parents. Two research instruments were used to examine the adjustment and absorption of Na'aleh students sent to kibbutzim: An adjustment scale examining social acceptance, practical problems, personal distress, and conflictual relationships; and a second scale that measured factors related to absorption in Israel: levels of satisfaction, willingness to live in Israel, coping with leaving the CIS, and desire to adopt an Israeli identity. Evidently, Na'aleh students in kibbutzim experienced fewer adjustment problems than those in state schools and more adjustment problems than those sent to religious schools. Kibbutz intakes suffered greater personal distress than Na'aleh intakes in non-kibbutz schools. Distress took the form of social alienation, sense of lack of control and confusion. The article seeks to understand the kibbutz's unique contribution to the project and its difficulties regarding the absorption of Na'aleh students in Israel. *[Article copies available for a fee from The Haworth Document Delivery Service: 1-800-342-9678. E-mail address: <getinfo@haworthpressinc.com> Website: <http://www.HaworthPress.com> © 2001 by The Haworth Press, Inc. All rights reserved.]*

This article is based on the findings of a study commissioned by the Association for Advancement in Education and conducted by the Szold Institute. The study dealt with the acclimatization and absorption of Na'aleh students in Israel (Bendas-Jacob & Friedman, 1996).

[Haworth co-indexing entry note]: "One Russian 'Chevrat Noar' Group in the Kibbutz: An Assessment of the Na'aleh Program." Bendas-Jacob, Orit. Co-published simultaneously in *Child & Youth Services* (The Haworth Press, Inc.) Vol. 22, No. 1/2, 2001, pp. 93-112; and: *Innovative Approaches in Working with Children and Youth: New Lessons from the Kibbutz* (ed: Yuval Dror) The Haworth Press, Inc., 2001, pp. 93-112. Single or multiple copies of this article are available for a fee from The Haworth Document Delivery Service [1-800-342-9678, 9:00 a.m. - 5:00 p.m. (EST). E-mail address: getinfo@haworthpressinc.com].

KEYWORDS. Youth Aliyah, Confederation of Independent States, alienation, youth services, immigration, cross-cultural education, youth work, groupwork

Since the early 1990s, the kibbutz movement has been involved in the initial absorption of immigrants from the former Confederation of Independent States (CIS). A six-month absorption track known as "A First Home in the Homeland" was developed for families and individuals. Another track was developed later, known this time as "A Second Home in the Homeland," which made it possible for immigrant families and individuals to extend their stay in the kibbutz. In addition, there were Hebrew language courses and direct absorption tracks for those who wished to join the kibbutz. Young people who had left their parents due to family or circumstantial reasons were accepted by kibbutzim through Chevrat Noar groups organized by the Youth Aliyah[1] section of the Jewish Agency. These youngsters were welcomed by the kibbutz community and lived there throughout their youth (Moyne, Palgi and Orhan, 1994; Shlaski, 1997). With the inception of the Na'aleh project, designed to bring youth from the CIS to Israel without their parents, the project founders hoped that some would be absorbed by kibbutzim, like families in the Chevrat Noar model. Lessons from the Na'aleh experience may be useful to those interested in youth immigration processes and to educators interested in dormitory life in general where students have to cope without the immediate support of their families.

THE NA'ALEH PROJECT

Na'aleh (Hebrew acronym for "Youth Immigrating Without Their Parents") is a national project that arranges for youth groups from the CIS to emigrate to Israel without their parents to pursue their education. The idea of bringing groups of young people from the CIS to Israel without their parents began in the early 1990s. It was conceived by the Liaison Office, an Israel office operating in the CIS on behalf of the state of Israel, in response to the large numbers of inquiries the office received from Jewish parents. These parents were interested in helping their children escape the economic hardships and growing uncertainty in the CIS and in helping them acquire a high standard of education.

The Liaison Office discovered that parents in Belorussia, Ukraine, and Russia were very willing to send their children to Israel to study. Liaison Office representatives saw the immigration of youth without parents as a new and important way of augmenting the immigrant pool, a pool that had been mostly families. The Jewish Agency board approached then Prime Minister Yitzhak Shamir, and the Project was approved in principle. Soon the Na'aleh project was launched as a collaborative project between the Ministry of Education and Culture, the Ministry of Immigration and Absorption, and the CIS Liaison Office. After carefully screening applicants for their emotional and intellectual abilities, the project selected a group of 15-year-old youth to join the selective–and therefore prestigious–three-year state study program.

The youth professional focus of the Na'aleh Project took into account the effect of separating adolescents from their parents and the culture shock they would experience upon arrival in Israel. Fifteen is an appropriate age to separate parents and children, since the individual begins to experience psychological separation from his or her parents. However, a separation that has not been properly processed may prove harmful. Since not everyone is suited to such a program, the Na'aleh organizers recommended that those who did not meet screening criterion should emigrate with their parents through other programs. To avoid emotional damage or developmental disturbance, strict candidate selection procedures were designed that mostly emphasized emotional maturity, relatively strong motivation, ability to separate from parents, ability to adapt socially, absence of any psychopathology, and the personal strength needed to handle problems and crises. No student was accepted to the Na'aleh program without the prior approval of a psychologist.

It was assumed that a program such as Na'aleh would entail conditions of stress and crisis even for the stronger students with normative personalities. A therapeutic absorption policy was therefore developed and a support system made available to students throughout the program. The program tried to address each student individually during the screening process, the preparatory Hebrew language course, on arrival at the airport, and when they needed to contact their parents. The organizers wished to provide support and to engender a sense of belonging and identity. They developed a system of support comprised of group instructors, tutors, housemother, social workers, and project administrators. Host families and school principals who were personally involved provided a further support network. The idea of the "Na'aleh Family" was introduced to describe the collaborative efforts of the teams, parents, and children. Despite the fact that the institutions involved in the project were widely distributed around the country, efforts were made to help them feel a part of the project network and to help

Na'aleh students maintain contact with one another. The psychological objective was to create a sense of "unit pride" as a means of increasing motivation and improving the participants' feeling of well-being.

In November, 1992, most of the first group of Na'aleh students arrived in Israel. Mrs. Shulamit Aloni, then Minister of Education and Culture, welcomed the new arrivals and the assembled guests experienced a sense of "pioneering Zionist groundbreaking." Of the 336 students who began the first year, 332 completed it. The following year, prime minister Yitzhak Rabin welcomed the second Na'aleh group with a sentence that has since appeared at the bottom of the stationery used by the Na'aleh administration: "There is no loftier (*Na'aleh* means "lofty" in Hebrew) endeavor than *Na'aleh!*"

In the first year, most Na'aleh students were referred to residential schools not affiliated with kibbutzim. In the second, kibbutz schools joined the absorption effort. About 43% of the students in the second Na'aleh cohort were sent to schools in the kibbutzim: Sasa, Evron, Beit-Alpha, Shefayim, Nir-Oz, Kerem-Shalom, Kfar Rupin, Maoz-Haim, Kfar Masaryk, Gonen, Mizra and Bror-Hayil. Only the school at Ein-Shemer, Mevo'ot-Eiron, enrolled students in the first cohort as well.

NA'ALEH STUDENTS IN KIBBUTZIM: A STUDY OF ADJUSTMENT

The aim of the study reported here was to explore two aspects of adjustment to life in Israel as experienced by the first Na'aleh kibbutz groups: educational and social adaptation and overall adjustment to the country. By comparing kibbutz schools to non-kibbutz schools, we wished to discover whether the kibbutz had any unique characteristics that affected the students' adaptation and adjustment. We further wished to suggest directions in which the kibbutz might be able to provide a more supportive environment for groups such as Na'aleh.

The sample comprised 238 Na'aleh students at the end of their second year in Israel who were studying in kibbutz schools. (This represented approximately 84% of the entire Na'aleh kibbutz student population at the time of the study.) The comparison group contained 177 Na'aleh students from the same cohort who were studying in other schools: 69 in state schools and 102 in religious state schools.

Two assessment scales were constructed: the Friedben scale of school adaptation and the Friedben scale for absorption in Israel (see

Appendix). Both scales contain positive and negative statements. Measures relating to the degree of adaptation were indicative of adjustment difficulties, while the absorption scale addressed attitudes toward Israel and willingness to live in the country. The adaptation scale indices were (a) lack of social acceptance, (b) personal distress, (c) interpersonal conflict, and (d) difficulties at school and in the dormitory.

The absorption scale indices were (a) satisfaction with Israel, (b) willingness to settle in the country, (c) coping with being uprooted from the CIS, and (d) assuming Israeli identity. Besides the quantitative aspects, students were asked to respond to open-ended questions, and tutors, principals, and the support team were asked to complete questionnaires. The major results of the study are presented here.

STUDENT RESPONSES

"I Felt a Need to Change My Life"

Students offered various explanations for their decision to join the Na'aleh program: a desire to abandon the CIS and to use the Na'aleh program to emigrate to Israel and thus accelerate their parents' immigration, or a wish to get away from their parents. Those who saw Israel as attractive because it is a Jewish country were largely those who had suffered anti-semitism or who were drawn towards Judaism: "I wanted to make *Aliyah* to the promised land like the people I read about in the *Mishnah*." However, the main reason for agreeing to join Na'aleh was the wish for greater opportunities, new experiences, and independence.

Fears about the program focused naturally on separation from parents and friends. The students feared homesickness and lack of support, social problems, and difficulties in adapting to the new environment. "I was worried about leaving my mother, I was afraid that the separation would drain my strength." Among the concerns about moving to a foreign country about which they knew relatively little were the climate, the sun, security, the secular population, the different mentality, and their education. They were concerned about their ability to cope with school and afraid of failure. They worried also about rejection and loneliness: not being able to make friends, the group not being nice, getting into Israeli society, and "What it's like living with kids you never met." Old fears were also restored. "I always had a hard time with getting on with people."

The students were also concerned that the program would not match the expectations created by Na'aleh representatives. "Even in the language course they presented us with a lot of propaganda, but I didn't really believe it. I knew that nothing could be as wonderful as they described." However, some of them were swept away by unrealistic expectations. "My expectations were in line with my age; in other words, I was looking for something that didn't exist; you might call it a fantasy." Reality for these teenagers came as a rude awakening and hindered their integration.

Upon their arrival in Israel, the Na'aleh group underwent considerable adjustment problems pertaining to dormitory and school life, coping with the dynamics of living in a closed group, severe homesickness, a different climate, alienation from Israeli society, problems concerning social rejection, and the need to cope with kibbutz life. The transition to a new culture raised fears of loss of identity and loss of roots. These cumulative problems ultimately produced emotional distress.

About half the students were not very pleased with their studies, while almost a third reported that they were bored in class or said that studies were oppressive. About one-fourth said they had difficulty adjusting to school discipline and some reported alienation from the teachers, saying they felt discriminated against by teachers. Na'aleh students in kibbutz schools reported a lack of social acceptance. Only one-half of the students reported satisfaction with the social situation or reported having a lot of influence in class. About one-fourth doubted having the full cooperation of students in their class. More than one-third reported making superficial social contacts.

Regarding coping with being uprooted from the CIS, one-half of the students said they were afraid of losing touch with their families in the CIS, and about one-third reported severe homesickness for friends in the CIS. Two-thirds said they were scared of losing touch with their roots or said they were concerned about being swallowed up by Israeli culture. "It's hard being without a family or a home." "It's hard not having mom's cooking." "There's no one there to encourage you the way it was at home." "I have nothing besides school."

Personal distress reported by Na'aleh students in the kibbutz schools took several forms. Almost one-third of the students reported that they often felt depressed and lonely. Around 40% reported feeling a lack of control over their lives, confusion, not having found their place, and feeling "left out." About one-fourth reported difficulties in communicating with others. Some even had trouble adjusting to the kibbutz. "In the kibbutz, social pressure is a problem." "There's a lot of gossip."

"It's boring here." "I don't like the aloof behavior of the kibbutz people."

"When I Learned a Bit About the Holocaust I Had No Doubt that I Wanted to Live Here"

Despite these problems and their distress, a majority of the Na'aleh students reported that they were satisfied with both Israel and the program and wanted to live in the country and become part of its society. Satisfaction with Israel was usually described in general terms as success, "fitting in," well-being, and personal growth. More than half said they were happy in Israel, happy with the school and dormitory, that their expectations had been fulfilled, that their program of studies suited them, and that they identified with the school's orientation. They also reported their participation in the program as a personal success and experienced a sense of freedom.

A willingness to settle in Israel was reflected in statements of intent, attitudes, and a commitment to become part of the country. More than two-thirds of the students said they would like to stay in Israel after the program. Over half reported that it was important for them to integrate in Israel and become part of society and that they were willing to undergo considerable hardship to make Israel their home.

Assuming an Israeli identity was reflected in the way students evaluated how far they had advanced in the integration process. A little less than one-half reported that they felt they had reached the end of a process of integration and adaptation to the country. A little over one-half reported feeling there was still a long way ahead of them until they were integrated or felt they would never truly be Israelis.

The cited accomplishments toward integration into Israel were a knowledge of Jewish history, the land, and–most of all–developing close relations with Israelis. Having Israeli friends, admirers, an adoptive kibbutz family are signs that the community cares about them.

When the Na'aleh group was taken to visit historic sites, it helped them identify with the country and directly affected their willingness to be in the country. "Not long ago we went to Kibbutz Lochamei HaGetaot (kibbutz named after fighters in ghetto uprisings) and saw an exhibition about young people who came to Israel and built up the land. I saw what they had been through, and I suddenly realized that my problems were nothing compared to theirs and that I should stay positive and stop making a fuss."

Some students saw their participation in joint projects together with Israelis and in social activities as something that affected the wider Israeli-Russian context. "We were in a camp outside town. They divided us into mixed groups (immigrants and veteran Israelis). It was really important that the Israelis had a chance to find out that we also knew how to work." The social factor was seen as extremely important and a major contribution to integration: "I fell in love! I've got some really close friends; it's easy to talk to Israelis and understand them." "I made friends with a few Israelis–they're great."

Ultimately, the Na'aleh students felt that events of significance to their integration were those that had to do with the inner change they achieved: "I stopped seeing everything in terms of my problems and realized I am strong enough to overcome most of the difficulties I encounter."

COMPARISONS BETWEEN NA'ALEH STUDENTS IN KIBBUTZ SCHOOLS AND NON-KIBBUTZ SCHOOLS

We compared the scores for kibbutz and non-kibbutz schools in the religious and non-religious sectors in Israel. Three main findings are noteworthy:

1. It was harder for Na'aleh students in the non-kibbutz, secular state schools to adapt to school life than their peers in the kibbutz schools. More of the Na'aleh students in non-kibbutz schools reported having difficulties with the dormitory and the school than the Na'aleh students in kibbutz schools. It should be emphasized that although the difference was statistically significant, it was not large. No statistically significant correlation was found between kibbutz and non-kibbutz schools in the secular system regarding absorption in Israel.

2. When secular, state kibbutz schools were compared with non-kibbutz, religious state schools, it was found that the students in the kibbutz schools experienced more difficulty in adapting to school than those studying in the non-kibbutz, religious state schools. Na'aleh students studying on the kibbutz reported a lack of social acceptance and personal distress more often than those in the religious, state schools. Further, the comparison showed that more Na'aleh students in the religious state schools reported feeling absorbed into the country than their peers in the kibbutz school system. This difference emerged from the following factors, which

were reported more frequently by Na'aleh students in the religious state schools than those in the kibbutz school system: contentment in Israel with a willingness to settle in the country and to assume Israeli identity. Here too the difference was also statistically significant but not great.

3. The comparison between kibbutz and non-kibbutz schools regardless of their orientation shows that Na'aleh students studying in kibbutz schools more frequently experienced adaptation difficulties than those in non-kibbutz schools. This was due to personal distress. Here too the difference was statistically significant but not great. No statistically significant difference was found between type of school (kibbutz or non-kibbutz) and student absorption in Israel.

The main differences between the kibbutz and non-kibbutz students are exemplified by the following: 41% of the kibbutz students reported a lack of control over their lives compared with 27% of the non-kibbutz students. Forty-five percent of kibbutz students reported often feeling "left out" compared with 35% of the non-kibbutz students. Twenty-four percent of the kibbutz students found it difficult to communicate with other people compared with 13% of the non-kibbutz students. More students in kibbutzim felt alone, confused, had a sense of failure, and reported dependency on their instructors than non-kibbutz students.

We can learn several lessons from the findings of the present study regarding kibbutz achievements in integrating Na'aleh students, adaptation difficulties experienced by Na'aleh students studying in kibbutzim, and differences between secular and religious state schools.

KIBBUTZ ACHIEVEMENTS
IN INTEGRATING NA'ALEH STUDENTS

About two-thirds of the Na'aleh students who stayed in kibbutzim were prepared to settle in Israel. Over one-half of the Na'aleh students who stayed in kibbutzim reported feeling satisfied with life in Israel and described their life here as a success.

The Na'aleh students who participated in this study were at the end of their second year in Israel, and the findings detailed above must be considered in the light of existing immigration models. According to such models, time is a crucial variable affecting the adaptation and integration of immigrants to a new country (Dotan and Shapir, 1992; Mirsky, 1996; Mirsky and Prawer, 1992). One of the models mentioned by

Mirsky and Prawer places the process of emotional adaptation experienced by immigrants along a time line with three main stages.

Stage I is characterized by emotional and cognitive overload and the euphoria and idealization of the new country due to an illusion that the future will be better than the old reality. Stage 2 involves a more sober, realistic assessment than the first impression. The immigrant becomes aware of the limitations of his new home and of himself in it and of the need to cope with the new reality. For these reasons, immigrants often feel a lack of control, introversion, passivity, and nostalgia. They often regret their decision to immigrate and adopt a self-critical, self-accusatory, angry stance toward both themselves and people around them. Often the frustration and conflict experienced during Stage 2 appears to be linked directly to the discrepancy between their expectations and reality. Stage 3 is the stage of integration. As the individual shows increasing ability to cope and gradually connects with life around him, a sense of belonging and identification with the new country can be seen. At this point success will depend on how effectively the individual manages to integrate his or her previous identity with the new one. As satisfaction grows, there is an improvement in day-to-day functioning and a significant reduction in the emotional distress symptoms that characterize the previous stage.

According to this model, the Na'aleh students in the kibbutzim had reached the end of the second stage by the time they became involved in this study. We may therefore expect them to exhibit a greater willingness to settle in Israel as time goes by. This speculation has been confirmed by the absorption scale scores of a sample drawn from the first cohort of Na'aleh students who were in their third year in the country at the time of this study. Their scores were statistically significantly higher than those of the second cohort. Among the items indicative of this trend were: "I feel Israeli." "I feel I have reached the end of the process of integrating and adjusting to life in Israel." "I am prepared to experience great difficulty in order to integrate." If further studies also show a positive correlation between the integration of the Na'aleh students and the three-stage adaptation model described above, this will strongly support the decision to make this a three-year program.

ADAPTATION DIFFICULTIES EXPERIENCED BY NA'ALEH STUDENTS STUDYING IN KIBBUTZIM

The Na'aleh students in general, particularly those who studied in kibbutzim, all reported difficulty in adapting to their new circumstances. The personal distress factor is an exceptional factor on the adaptation scale used in this research. Next to it on the scale are three other factors: social acceptance, interpersonal conflict, and problems with dormitory and school. These factors describe behavioral phenomenon, while the distress factor relates to "internal" feelings, some of which would be described as severe distress.

The emotional distress reported by the kibbutz students is associated with the sharp transition from the first to the second stage described in the adaptation model. It seems that the special circumstances surrounding the second Na'aleh cohort might have intensified the euphoria and idealization of the first stage. Members of the second Na'aleh cohort were greeted with tremendous excitement and an especially enthusiastic reception: They were met at the airport by the Prime Minister and senior Ministry of Education and Ministry of Absorption officials and enveloped in love and a sense of national excitement. This may well have obscured the fact that they were in fact on the threshold of a complex and difficult process. The students had great expectations and, as we learned from their comments regarding the preparatory process in the CIS, these expectations had not been tempered. The expectations on the part of those involved in their absorption were also high because of the stringent screening process applied to both the children and the absorbing schools and the high value attributed to the program. Under the circumstances, when they entered the inevitable second stage, it is hardly surprising that their spirits plunged from unrealistic exuberance to painful disillusionment. Their emotional distress mainly took the form of conflict, alienation, a sense of lack of control, and strong feelings of homesickness and second thoughts regarding the entire project:

> When I arrived, everything was wonderful, new. I was happy with everything, it was like a dream, but as time went by this feeling changed. I began to see reality for what it was, and it was not what I had expected. The conditions are no dream and being stuck in the kibbutz all the time made it worse. School is quite hard. It's difficult to do well in *bagrut* (matriculation examinations) and get into university. It was hard making new friends, because society is different, and as time goes by, you begin to see reality instead of dreams.

We found that the emotional distress of the Na'aleh students in the kibbutzim was statistically significantly higher due to social alienation and a general lack of orientation in comparison to the distress reported by others of the same cohort in non-kibbutz settings. This requires efforts to try and identify the possible link between characteristics typical of the kibbutz itself, the kibbutz style of absorption, and this phenomenon. For many years the kibbutz movement had taken on a central role in rising to national challenges by welcoming large groups of young people and offering them a home and an education within the kibbutz community. In this way the kibbutz movement bolstered its own status, made contact with other sectors of the population, and even sought to store up a suitable reserve for its own future development (Shlasky, 1997). On more than one occasion the kibbutz achieved these goals through a policy of "intensive socialization" and by having the entire community act as "an educating community." Kibbutz members were expected to set a personal example and newcomers were expected to immerse themselves in kibbutz life and thus absorb the community's norms and values (Kashti, 1998).

On their arrival at the kibbutzim and joining the kibbutz schools, Na'aleh students found themselves involved in the day-to-day routine of this unique community, exposing them to its lifestyle and beliefs and accepting the risk of criticism of their very way of life. Also, some students may have sensed that something was expected of them in return for the nurturing they were receiving: active participation in the community, conformity to kibbutz norms, and perhaps even joining the kibbutz in the future. The requirement of participating in kibbutz work, which caused friction between themselves and kibbutz members (who were not always understanding or sensitive to the legitimate difficulties Na'aleh students were experiencing), apparently placed an excessive emotional burden on the Na'aleh students and exacerbated their existing distress. It is also possible that individualistic students found it difficult to function in a relatively closed society, especially since the willingness of the multigenerational population to accept the youngsters was not consistent. Moreover, the kibbutz controlled the students' time and activities, and since the latter were not always interested in joining in the local social and cultural life, this caused further discontentment.

The relative passivity demonstrated by the Na'aleh students (Vered, 1996) and the fact that they kept to themselves might be connected to their position in the community:

> The kibbutz is run by a group of people who make all the decisions. Anyone who is not involved has less of a chance of influencing things . . . They treat the new people who are not members differently, taking them far less into consideration, so that the dif-

ference between the *kibbutznikim* and the non-members is very obvious. (Vered, 1996, p. 55, 61)

Criticism was also leveled at what was perceived as inequality in the distribution of work assignments. Despite the fact that from the kibbutz perspective work assignments were decided on a expedient basis (they had difficulty in assigning immigrants to jobs requiring prior experience), the Na'aleh group saw it as discriminatory and humiliating: "There is no equality; new immigrants and volunteers do all the dirty work" (Vered, 1996, p. 61).

Kibbutz education is characterized by the simultaneous dominance of the family, the community, the school, and a special emphasis on the peer group. Young kibbutzniks are thus raised to be pro-social and actively committed to parallel social systems. Regional kibbutz residential schools such as the Anne Frank Haven maintained close and dynamic contact with students' home kibbutz. Their educational orientation was such that students were expected to be involved in studies, work, and peer-group, self-government activities (Ben Peretz, Giladi, and Dror, 1992; Dror, 1995). In this setting the Na'aleh students may have had difficulty in adapting to the regional kibbutz education framework, since they were less committed to the various systems (the class, work, *Hevrat Hayeladim* [the self-governing peer group]) than their kibbutz-born counterparts. Moreover, they may also have viewed the close link between the different educational layers as an irksome and oppressive social supervision (Ben Peretz, Giladi, and Dror, 1992). Furthermore, regional kibbutz schools have excellent records in absorbing students in the "youth at risk" or lower SES categories and they were less experienced–at least in the first year when this research took place–in absorbing an elite group such as Na'aleh students who did not hesitate to criticize the system whenever they felt the need.

It seems that relative to their peers in schools outside the kibbutz framework, the Na'aleh students living on kibbutzim or who were educated in regional kibbutz schools were subjected to a more intensive socialization process and a firm but relatively flexible ideology (in contrast to the religious ideology). This study presents what emerged from direct reports made by the students and those involved in their absorption. To understand what produced these findings, further investigation of this subject is clearly needed. However, one should be alert to symptoms of emotional distress, and treatment measures should be in place on both the individual as well as group levels. We need to moderate our expectations of the students and allow them to find their own place in kibbutz society–at their own pace–while monitoring and evaluating their integration on a regular basis.

DIFFERENCES BETWEEN SECULAR AND RELIGIOUS STATE SCHOOLS

Na'aleh students who studied in religious schools were found to experience fewer social and educational adaptation difficulties, feel greater satisfaction with Israel, and show greater willingness to make the country theirs and assume Israeli identity. It seems that the difference stems from the fundamentally different things offered by the religious and secular schools. The religious schools provided Na'aleh student immigrants with an environment that offered a clear and committed way of life. The students had to cope with a stable spiritual worldview which, despite its relative strictness, is on the whole presented pleasingly and by way of personal example. Clear limits are set, and the religious experience to which the students are exposed in religious schools requires them to respond to a comprehensible and clear-cut reality. It was found that religious school teachers also had more influence on their students than teachers did in the secular school system. All these factors apparently helped students' internalization of their connection with the land and the Jewish tradition.

In our opinion the above finding, which relates to the issue of "secular" versus "religious" culture in Israel, goes beyond the subject of the study and therefore will not be discussed further here. However, given that within the secular sector, students who studied in kibbutzim were found to have adapted better to the country than those in non-kibbutz schools, perhaps this offers a possible direction for a secular Israeli culture to offer an identification model for populations that are not necessarily religious.

CONCLUSION

With regard to general issues regarding the absorption of immigrant youth in kibbutzim, we wish to reiterate that this study examines how well the first Na'aleh cohort in the kibbutzim had adjusted and been absorbed at the time when their problems were at their most severe. The problems described may be dealt with by moderating the expectations of all those involved in absorption (the immigrants and those absorbing them), by allocating resources for comprehensive professional support, and by being extremely alert to the students' emotional situation. The "family absorption" unique to kibbutzim is a vital source of emotional support, and, in our opinion, the families should also be provided with professional support.

It is essential to find ways of reinforcing students' personal strengths. The desire to be regarded as independent adults both in their own eyes and in the eyes of others was of primary importance to the students. Their desire for independence was one of the main reasons for joining the program and being able to overcome problems unaided was mentioned as something that facilitated their integration in Israel. Among the suggestions offered by the students for improving the adjustment of future Na'aleh groups was a personally tailored curriculum and also the opportunity to earn money independently (the money was not the main issue here). The students also said that they wished to travel around the country on their own. Therefore we believe that if Na'aleh students were allowed greater freedom of choice and independence during their absorption, this would increase their feeling of control over their own lives and contribute to their sense of personal responsibility for the process they are involved in. It would also contribute to the normative processes of shaping an independent identity that takes place in individuals of this age group.

In our opinion, we need to be satisfied with the fairly high level of the students' willingness to live in Israel and adopt an Israeli identity, and we should encourage efforts to help them identify with the country while preserving the unique qualities that these young people have to offer. In students' open reports, we see that they display self-awareness and a sense of determination to pursue the integration process. The wisdom of hindsight has allowed the Na'aleh kibbutz group to see the changes in themselves since their arrival in Israel. They have apparently experienced an accelerated maturation process whose results are quite obvious.

> Things have changed since I first arrived here: I began to see people in Israel differently, I started feeling Israeli and that I was part of this country, I started thinking more logically, and I lost some of my childhood illusions. I always try to understand why others behave the way they do and try to put myself in their place and figure out what's going on in their heads. I have started to be interested in other areas of art, and the most important thing is that I have fallen in love for the first time.

The project now involves some 2,600 students in three different age groups. About 40% are studying in kibbutz schools. We would recommend another follow-up study of the first cohort who have now completed their army service or their first university degree. We need to reappraise the integration and adaptation process being experienced by the Na'aleh students in the various kibbutzim (both religious and secular) and explore how their experiences have affected their lives.

NOTE

1. Youth Aliyah was founded in 1933 to rescue Jewish youth throughout Europe and since then has been serving as a facilitator of youth immigration from different countries. Youth Aliyah took part in the absorption and education of the newcomers. It specializes in boarding education: Schools, villages, and kibbutzim. For further information, see Kashti (1998).

AUTHOR NOTE

Orit Bendas-Jacob is a researcher in the Henrietta Szold Institute–The Israeli National Institute for Research in the Behavioral Sciences. Her fields of research are adolescents in social conflict, youth immigration to Israel from Russia and Ethiopia, test anxiety in adolescence and assessing social programs.

REFERENCES

Bendas-Jacob, O., & Friedman, I. A. (1996). *Na'aleh–Youth immigrating without their parents.* Jerusalem: Henrietta Szold Institute. (In Hebrew)
Ben Peretz, M., Giladi, M., & Dror, Y. (1992). The Anna Frank Haven: A case of an alternative educational program in an integrative kibbutz setting. *International Review of Education, 38* (1), 47-63.
Dotan, T., & Shapir, M. (1992). Psychological aspects of immigrant absorption. In R. Cohen (Ed.), *Between two worlds* (pp. 34-40). Jerusalem: Ministry of Education and Culture. (In Hebrew)
Dror, Y. (1995). The Anna Frank Haven in an Israeli Kibbutz. *Adolescence, 50* (119), 617-629.
Kashti, Y. (1998). Israeli youth village: Boarding schools in the service of nation-building. *Child & Youth Services, 19* (1), 55-78.
Kashti, Y., & Shalev, U. (1981). "Hakibbutz Ha'arzi" school as a socializing organization. *Eunim Bahinuch, 29,* 34-40. (In Hebrew)

Mirsky, J. (1996). Psychological aspects of immigration: Literature review. *Psychology*, 5 (2), 199-214. (In Hebrew)

Mirsky, J., & Prawer, L. (1992). *To immigrate as an adolescent: Immigrant youth from the former Soviet Union in Israel*. Jerusalem: Van Leer Institute. (In Hebrew)

Moyne, V., Palgi, M., & Orhan, E. (1994). *The contribution of the kibbutz to absorbing immigrants from the CIS*. Haifa: University of Haifa. (In Hebrew)

Shlasky, S. (1997). Kibbutz identity in the mirror of "Hevrat-Hanoar." In Y. Dror (Ed.), *Kibbutz education in its environment* (pp. 189-221). Tel Aviv, Israel: Tel Aviv University. (In Hebrew)

Vered, N. (1996). *Na'aleh's democratic conceptualization*. Unpublished master's thesis, The Hebrew University of Jerusalem. (In Hebrew)

APPENDIX A

FRIEDBEN ADJUSTMENT TO SCHOOL SCALE AND THE FRIEDBEN ABSORPTION IN ISRAEL SCALE

Factor Structure for the Friedben Adaptation to School Scale Scale α = .88.

FACTOR I–Personal Distress (α = .79)

I feel lonely.
I have got quite a few personal problems.
I often feel depressed.
I often feel I lack control over my life.
I have difficulty communicating with others around me.
I feel confused, I haven't settled in yet.
I often feel left out.
Aliyah has greatly disrupted my inner equilibrium.
I try to make friends but others reject me.
I feel socially rejected.
Others think I'm stupid because I can't express myself properly in Hebrew.

FACTOR II–Lack of Social Acceptance (α = .74)

I feel that people like me. (R)
I join in a lot of cultural activity. (R)

I get very good cooperation from the students in my class. (R)
I am popular in my class. (R)
Students in class help me whenever necessary. (R)
I have very good cooperation from students in the dormitory who are not in my class. (R)
I am very pleased with my social situation. (R)
I have considerable influence in my class. (R)
My social relationships are superficial.

Note: Items marked (R) were coded in reverse

FACTOR III–Interpersonal Conflict (α = .63)

I have been involved in incidents of physical violence.
I get involved in lots of confrontations with non-*Na'aleh* immigrant students.
I am involved in lots of confrontations with *Na'aleh* students.
I am in conflict with the teachers.
I have been involved in verbally violent incidents.
I get involved in lots of confrontations with Israeli students.
Before I immigrated to Israel I had social problems at school.

FACTOR IV–Difficulties at School (α = .73)

I have problems with dormitory discipline.
The dormitory living conditions are very uncomfortable.
I have problems with school discipline.
I find the studying boring.
I am satisfied with the dormitory. (R)
Relations with the teachers are cold.
I feel the teachers deprive me.
Studying aggravates me.
There is complete understanding between the teachers and me. (R)
I am very satisfied with my academic situation. (R)

APPENDIX B

Factor Structure for the Friedben Absorption in Israel Scale Scale ∝ = .8270.

Factor I–Satisfaction with Israel (∝ = .82)

Overall, I feel good at school.
Overall, I feel good in the dormitory.
Overall, I feel good in Israel.
Na'aleh is a success for me.
My hopes regarding life in Israel have come true.
The academic course suits me.
Na'aleh has led to my personal growth.
I identify with the path the school offers me.
I feel free in Israel.
I think I will complete my matriculation as planned and with success.

FACTOR II–Willingness to Settle in the Country (α = .77)

I would like to stay in Israel after the program.
I am considering returning to the CIS after the program. (R)
With hindsight, the decision to join *Na'aleh* was the right one.
I want to integrate within Israeli society.
It is important for me to be part of Israeli society.
I regret my coming to Israel. (R)
I am willing to undergo a lot of difficulty in order to integrate into Israeli society.
Moving to Israel has helped me mature and become more independent.
I would like to join the army.

FACTOR III-Coping with Being Uprooted from the CIS (α = .59)

I am afraid of losing my roots. (R)
I am afraid of losing touch my family in the CIS. (R)
I am afraid of being swallowed up by Israeli culture. (R)
I really miss my friends in the CIS. (R)

FACTOR IV–Assuming Israeli Identity (α = .56)

I feel Israeli.
I feel I have reached the end of the integration and adjustment process.
I feel there is still a long way to go before I am integrated into Israeli society. (R)
I feel I will never be truly Israeli. (R)
I speak Hebrew fluently.

Integration in Kibbutz Day Schools: Regionalization of Secondary and Elementary Schools in the Beit Shean Valley Since 1972

Yuval Dror

SUMMARY. Since the 1970s, many kibbutz educational systems have moved from schools solely for one kibbutz to regional schools. Regional schools put the kibbutzim goal of maintaining their own uniqueness in tension with their need and desire to integrate with and contribute to Israeli society. Consolidation required attention to the differing educational abilities and capacities of diverse students and redefining community in heterogeneous, regional terms. These have benefited participating kibbutzim and, based on traditional strengths of kibbutz education, these regional schools have contributed principles of non-selective (inclusive) education, community and classroom values education, and acceptance of difference in others. Integration in regional schools requires schools to adapt to the diversity of the region but also to the uniqueness of participating communities. *[Article copies available for a fee from The Haworth Document Delivery Service: 1-800-342-9678. E-mail address: <getinfo@haworthpressinc.com> Website: <http://www.HaworthPress.com> © 2001 by The Haworth Press, Inc. All rights reserved.]*

KEYWORDS. Regional schools, kibbutz education, kibbutz movement, moshav, elementary and secondary education, school autonomy

Yuval Dror is affiliated with Tel-Aviv University and Oranim.

[Haworth co-indexing entry note]: "Integration in Kibbutz Day Schools: Regionalization of Secondary and Elementary Schools in the Beit Shean Valley Since 1972." Dror, Yuval. Co-published simultaneously in *Child & Youth Services* (The Haworth Press, Inc.) Vol. 22, No. 1/2, 2001, pp. 113-133; and: *Innovative Approaches in Working with Children and Youth: New Lessons from the Kibbutz* (ed: Yuval Dror) The Haworth Press, Inc., 2001, pp. 113-133. Single or multiple copies of this article are available for a fee from The Haworth Document Delivery Service [1-800-342-9678, 9:00 a.m. - 5:00 p.m. (EST). E-mail address: getinfo@haworthpressinc.com].

113

THE HISTORY OF KIBBUTZ SCHOOLS:
FROM EXCLUSIVENESS TO INCLUSION

This research is a historical case study of educational integration–by economic level–in the regional day schools of the kibbutz movement. From the early 1970s onwards almost all the kibbutz elementary and secondary schools are organized in regional kibbutz (and moshav[1]) schools throughout the country; except for 10 boarding schools, the majority of them are day schools.

The Neveh Eitan Regional Secondary School in the Beit Shean Valley began integration processes as part of the reform in Israel's educational structure, after frustration in the wake of two earlier attempts to handle the problem of educational deprivation. One attempt was on the principle of mechanical equality (the same curricula, methods, and examinations for all the pupils–both high and low achievers). The other attempt was based on "compensatory education." In 1968, Israel's parliament–the Knesset–extended compulsory education to grade 9 and reorganized the system into three divisions: elementary school from grades 1 to 6, intermediate school from grades 7 to 9, and senior school from grades 10 to 12. Intermediate school districts were to be remapped to integrate children from the stronger socioeconomic levels of the Israeli society with those from the weaker ones, so that the latter would be better prepared for senior school and eventually gain access to higher education. Another type of integration was between children from the relatively old kibbutzim, established in the 1930s and 1940s by people from Israel, Europe, and America, with moshav children whose parents came as part of the mass immigration of the 1950s and 1960s.

The study commenced in the 1972 to 1973 school year in the Beit Shean Valley Cooperative, Beit Chinuch Neveh Eitan.[2] In the last 25 years integrative education for kibbutz and moshav children has become firmly established and since 1986 has come to include the elementary school. In general this is a success story followed and documented by research–despite difficulties that persist to this day.

The Beit Shean Valley is a characteristic region of kibbutz and moshav settlement, opened in the Wall and Watchtower era (1936-1939) as part of the struggle against the British plan to divide *Eretz Israel* (Mandatory Palestine) into what were then the Jewish and Arab areas. The Beit Shean kibbutzim and moshavim Jewish population was homogeneous. The large majority were graduates of either local youth movements or of those in Europe and America. The children went to elementary school in their own kibbutzim and moshavim and, when the kibbutz children grew to secondary school age in the late 1940s, to one of three secondary schools–one for each kibbutz movement. The religious kibbutzim had day schools, the leftist Kibbutz Ha'rtzi a residential school–not discussed in this article–and Hever Hakvutzot (hereafter Ihud Hakvutzot v'Hakibutzim) had a day school at Kibbutz Neveh Eitan. At first, Neveh Eitan secondary school was attended only by its own children and those of Kibbutz Kfar Ruppin but later, in the 1950s, also by children from Kibbutz Hamadia. In 1968, Maoz Haim of Hakibbutz Hameuhad movement joined Neveh Eitan secondary school, making a great practical and ideological concession in giving up its local elementary and secondary school, because it had too few students and teachers. In the early 1970s Hakibbutz Hameuhad children from Neveh Ur came in, and the moshav children followed in 1972 as a result of remapping districts.

The first two moshavim in the area disbanded before 1948, the year Israel became a state. After that five new moshavim in the northern and southern sections of the Beit Shean Valley were settled by people from Kurdistan, many from remote mountain areas of their native country. They went to local National Religious elementary schools and those from the three southern moshavim continued at the nearby secondary school of the religious kibbutzim at Sdeh Eliahu. The majority of the settlers in the two northern moshavim were secular, though traditional in life-style, and most of their children attended the national special education elementary school at Moshav Yardena. This was staffed largely by "soldier teachers": Women conscripts sent by the army for a single year after a few months of training. For years the few children of secondary school age had no suitable school in the region until the intermediate division at Neveh Eitan set up in the 1972 to 1973 school year provided one.

This article presents the case history of the intermediate division then established in the Beit Shean Valley and continues with the development of the integrative elementary school that began to function in the following decade. Research findings on integration will be presented briefly in chronological order. These will be interpreted by means of the theoretical "size dilemma model" for kibbutz schools. The "local regionalism" dimension will be prominent in the analysis, since the degree of success of integration is the result of adaptation to local conditions.

THE SIZE DILEMMA MODEL:
A NARRATIVE REVIEW

This study is based on a review of four historical studies and follow-up research carried out in the Beit Shean Valley. The five researchers are kibbutz members who were principals of the schools under discussion, although not all held the position at the time of the research nor did they investigate the schools they directed. They studied integration by means of learning achievement data, attitude questionnaires (some of which were compared to national findings), and open-ended questions. Three studies related to the earlier integration of the secondary school. Amnon Eitan's master's thesis, "The Interaction between Moshav and Kibbutz Children in the Intermediate Division in Neveh Eitan" (1975), is from the first three years. Two follow-ups of the study were carried out in 1986 by Rahel Noy and Margalit Kostrinsky, and in 1995 by Ettie Gonen and David Glazner, who did graduation projects on the subject for principals' courses at Oranim Teachers' College and the Hebrew University School of Education, respectively. Glazner (1996), in "The Development of Integration in Dekalim School in Beit Shean Valley," documented the process begun ten years earlier and analyzed it by means of interviews. The projects in the principals' courses were guided by me, an educational historian at Tel Aviv University, member of a Beit Shean Valley kibbutz, and part-time teacher at Neveh Eitan for several years.

Study of educational integration in Israel followed theories accepted in the field, particularly in the United States. These theories suggest that school structure carries a message beyond that of actual teaching, so that structural changes help to integrate the children of stronger and weaker social strata–both academically and socially. Home background is the most important factor in determining scholastic success, and the most important factor in the school setting is the nature of the other students. (Success is possible in heterogeneous classes, but in homogeneous weak classes it is not.) The social composition of a class affects students' attitudes towards themselves, classmates, and society as a whole. An integrated framework in itself is not enough, and social relationships must be nurtured deliberately in integrative classes.

These theories were examined in the Neveh Eitan secondary school and validated, despite the difficulties, over the years. In our historical description we mention only the principal findings, since we intend to introduce new material on educational integration, adding both theoretical and application dimensions to existing theories.

The first step was developing "the size dilemma model" for kibbutz regional schools, and it has been updated several times since 1986. The model is based on Niv and Bar-on's (1992) assumption that the kibbutz lives continuously the dilemma of maintaining its uniqueness, within closed internal frameworks, against its need and desire to integrate into the Israeli society. While it would like to be a small, intimate framework, it is required to cooperate with larger ones in its region, since it is not self-sufficient in such areas as agriculture, industry, education, and social and psychological services. Decisions to set up or expand regional schools were made in the 1950s and were considered subsequently in order to determine policy regarding variables that lie between the two poles: the classic kibbutz school–unique and autonomous–and the changing school that seeks to integrate with its surroundings. The schematic model is shown in Table 1.

TABLE 1. Comparison Between Autonomous and Integrated Kibbutz Schools

	Autonomous, Kibbutz Secondary School	Kibbutz Schools Integrated by Region and Students
Uniqueness	Entirely unique kibbutz education (methods, content, graduates)	Complete similarity to non-kibbutz education (methods, content, graduates)
Autonomy	A school in each kibbutz, kibbutz teachers and pupils	Complete integration of kibbutz teachers and pupils into neighboring, non-kibbutz regional or urban school
Size	Small kibbutz school (200-300 average)	Large regional school (700-800 average)
Integration	Integration into the socio-economic level parallel to the kibbutz	Integration with weaker socio-economic levels, from the so-called "The Other Israel"
Comprehensiveness	Academic studies in the humanities and sciences	Comprehensive school including a range of technological options
Totality	A comprehensive residential school where education comprises formal and nonformal elements, kibbutz centered	A day school where most of the education given is formal; has affinity to the society around it
Local-regionalism	A regional secondary school of each kibbutz movement	A regional school as a part of larger community, integrated with neighboring schools as to local circumstances

(Adapted from Dror, 1999, p. 123)

The two latest updates in the model (Dror, 1995; 1999) were the result of rapid changes in the Kibbutz Artzi residential educational institutions, some of which have become day schools. As a result, the Totality variable was introduced. It is not relevant, however, to our present discussion of day schools. But the "local regionalism" variable, applied to Kibbutz Artzi residential schools, is also applicable to kibbutz day schools. Historical material and follow-up data shows how the Beit Shean Valley schools grew, became more "comprehensive" academically, and, though they took in outside populations, retained their kibbutz "autonomy." These three self-evident variables represent no special innovation for the present study. The size dilemma as integration developed in the Beit Shean Valley revolved around other variables. The traditional kibbutz sense of "uniqueness" worked against involvement with other groups which interfered with education for kibbutz life. "Integration" became part of the social and educational consciousness of the kibbutz movement in the 1960s, undermining the historical sense of uniqueness. It was the local regionalism variable that swung the balance in favor of integration as against uniqueness: The need to consider regional conditions in the Beit Shean Valley dictated the particular path that integration took there.

THE SECONDARY SCHOOL BEIT HINUCH
AT NEVEH EITAN

The Intermediate Division's First Three Years (1972-1975)

Ministry of Education policy, as previously explained, supported the decision to open the intermediate division. It was relatively easy in the moshavim, since they were in such great educational difficulties: In the kibbutz, despite the problems, there was ideological motivation to make the move. From its inception, the kibbutz tried to educate its children to join the collective, so that curricula had special content that included daily physical work. The basic assumption was that behavior norms and the tie to the kibbutz home would be acquired in single-age groups of kibbutz peers under the guidance of teachers from the kibbutz and of leaders from the youth movements which, ideally, would function in every kibbutz. Because there were too few children and too many economic exigencies, however, regional (usually secondary) schools began to emerge as early as the 1930s. It was assumed that they would serve only the children of one kibbutz movement. It was a far-reaching compromise when Ihud admitted children from other movements in regions where there were few kibbutzim. All agreed that every kibbutz should have its own elementary school, and Hakibbutz Hameuhad favored a secondary school as the center of each such "educating community."

When regionalization was first discussed at kibbutz general meetings, there were reservations, but the support of the Neveh Eitan administration for the idea led to its acceptance. In the 1950s and 1960s there were fewer that 100 students in the Neveh Eitan school, and a survey predicted that only a few dozen more would come in from the kibbutzim in the foreseeable future. Joining the larger Ein Harod regional school with its vocational options was considered, but the kibbutzim preferred to keep the children nearer home, so they established an intermediate division that would take in the children of Beit Yosef and Yardena. The school doubled in size, and the motives were pragmatic: Support from the Ministry of Education would increase substantially. From an ideological point of view, the kibbutzim had a duty to come out of their own enclave and help the children of their neighbors who were part of "the other Israel" and to acquaint their own children with an important part of the Israeli demographic scene: the "eastern Jews" from the moshavim.

Preparations were made among kibbutz and moshav children for the first school year in 1971. The secondary school teachers from Neveh Eitan met with the moshav children and their teachers in an effort to develop a curriculum and demanding a psychological test for children in the special education class to determine how to integrate them. For administrative reasons the test was not held and students were divided into two grade 7 classes without considering the learning difficulties that many of them had. Unsurprisingly, the result was a teaching and social nightmare that lasted a full year. There was not only a conspicuous gap between the two groups, but any kind of bridging was shown to be impossible in such indiscriminate "total integration."

Social relationships were weak from the outset and became worse when the moshav children felt they were being deprived. There were taunts, violent vocal outbursts, and even physical blows in class and during recess. Moshav children and their parents perceived the organized tutoring after school hours as punishment and discrimination. One long school day for academic reinforcement a week was then arranged for all the children in grade 7, including those from the kibbutzim, which helped improve social relationships. The school administration campaigned among the moshav parents to persuade them to buy basic reference books for use at home. Meetings, festivities, and excursions were organized and proved to be socially effective. Another problem of the first year was that moshav children who integrated relatively well with those from the kibbutz found themselves isolated from friends at home.

Despite the small improvement, the first year of integration failed. In the second year, the incoming moshav children were given an achievement test in grade 6 after two-week preparatory classes in the summer taught by their new teachers. This became standard practice for the future. That same year, grade 8 placed 6th out of 19 in a nationwide academic achievement test carried out by Tel Aviv University! Social and other activities were fostered and considered successful by the students, including the Bar Mitzvah program. The kibbutz gave its own secular Jewish expression to the traditional male rite of passage at 13 years of age: It consisted of 13 individual and group tasks for boys and girls alike. They "transposed" this from the home kibbutz to the school where the moshav children participated also. The moshavim also staged a Bar Mitzvah performance in which the children summed up the year's achievements. From then on there was one in each moshav and kibbutz, and all students would attend each one. Despite the academic and social achievements, the modified selective policy of the second year–an "advancement class" for those needing special help–failed. Although kibbutz children who required it were also placed there, the moshav children and their parents again saw this too as deliberate discrimination. Also, it did not bring academic progress and caused wild behavior among the students. For these reasons the plan was dropped.

In the third year the middle way was finally found between the two integrative strategies. Special teaching hours were increased and homeroom time decreased. The basic social integration framework remained the heterogeneous homeroom class. In this third year after which the first integrative class was to graduate into senior high school, the school dealt with academic and social heterogeneity in a more informed manner. For prepared students, the educational advisor of the school guided them to continued academic studies at Neveh Eitan, while those having academic difficulties were directed to pre-military, residential vocational schools, after a preparatory year at the Beit Shean Comprehensive School, the only place in the region offering technological studies. Girls considering nursing school remained at Neveh Eitan for another year. Graduates of the special education class were directed to appropriate schools based on objective tests administered outside the school. The advisor involved each child from the moshavim, the parents, and their education committee in every individual decision made by Neveh

Eitan staff. Thus the first transfer to the senior division was accomplished. Lessons from the failure of social integration in the first year were carefully studied, and the third incoming class was integrated better than its predecessors. In a follow-up of the third year, the achievement gap between kibbutz and moshav children in mathematics, English, reading comprehension, and science had shrunk considerably from the 24% gap after grade 6, when the children had studied separately, to 12% after a year of going to school together. The children, including those who had been part of the violent encounter of the first year, reported significantly better social integration. Moreover, the "eastern" moshav children who might logically have been expected to feel deprived, evaluated social justice in Israel higher than did the "western" kibbutz children (in statistically absolute terms). The moshav children were significantly better satisfied with the school than the kibbutz children.

Eitan (1975) summed up the first three years of integration in the kibbutz-moshav school in the Beit Shean Valley as relatively successful. This was true particularly so from the moshav point of view. The kibbutz children tended to hold themselves aloof scholastically and socially in their new school, which may be attributed to the generally critical nature of the kibbutz as a small community and to the fact that they came from a stable, intimate, highly developed local school.

Most findings affirmed the basic assumptions of integration research in Israel and elsewhere. The learning achievements of the lower group improved without impairing those of the rest of the class. The "deprived" students from the moshav acquired more positive attitudes towards their classmates, school, and Israeli society in general, and they attended school willingly, something by no means taken for granted, because earlier they required the intervention of the truant officer. All graduates of the intermediate division, even those who dropped out over the years, continued studying in alternative institutions, a phenomenon previously unknown in the moshavim. The researcher credited the academic and particularly the social achievements to the unique, informal nature of the kibbutz school and to extracurricular social activity. This eventually brought about a true rapprochement not only between the moshavim children and their kibbutz peers but made the former more receptive to the academic demands of their teachers.

In contrast, Eitan describes the social costs to the moshav children in the tensions and mutual hostility they experienced at school, now diminished but not completely gone. Those absorbed academically and socially are now closer to the kibbutz children and more remote from those of the moshav. This is particularly true of those who transferred out of Neveh Eitan. Most of the girls dropped out of school, were isolated, and had very low self-awareness. There were, moreover, increased learning difficulties after grade 7. The "advancement class," for the lowest 25th percentile of the moshav children, failed and was replaced by a better one that combined tutoring with homeroom studies. Eitan concluded that learning problems must be addressed in elementary school and that social contacts should be started there, too. These conclusions were brought to the attention of the parties concerned, but ten years passed before the right conditions developed for an integrative elementary school.

Eitan examined and corroborated the "local community factor": the strong ties between the community and its educational system. Parents as community members feel responsibility and commitment to the system. This is the general idea behind many elementary schools and community schools through the secondary level. Eitan finds that local interest determines the success of integration between ethnic communities as exemplified by the kibbutzim and moshavim in the Beit Shean Valley–despite the problems and social costs.

The Noy-Kostrinsky Follow-Up Study (1986)

When the authors re-examined integration in the Neveh Eitan Cooperative Beit Hinuch, a decade later, it had 250 students. Noy was principal of Dekalim Elementary School which, at the time, refused to take grade 1 children from the moshavim. (That same year they were admitted to another school in the region, which later became part of Dekalim.) Kostrinsky was principal of Neveh Eitan, and during Amnon Eitan's study in 1975 headed its intermediate division. The authors described general changes during the decade: The economic situation in the moshavim was fair to good, most families either built new homes or renovated old ones, exteriors were landscaped, and the young people, many of them Beit Hinuch graduates, understood the importance of education. In many families, mothers worked outside the home. There are contacts with kibbutz members in employment and in cultural and social contexts in the region, including Bar Mitzvah celebrations. The moshav National Religious school closed, and the younger families tended to be more secular. Against this background, junior division achievements in mathematics, English, language, and science were examined again, and Amnon Eitan's questions were used again in an attitude questionnaire and in interviews with current students and graduates.

Ethnic communities were closer, though it fell short of a revolutionary change, and on the margins problems persisted. The educational gap still existed in 1986 but continued to decrease. A technology option for those having academic difficulties was opened in 1983. Parents no longer needed to be urged to buy reference books: They already had them. Kibbutz children and parents were less aware than their moshav counterparts, even at this time, how important integration was for them. A sense of the school as part of the regional community was even stronger than it was in the past among graduates and their parents. Noy and Kostrinsky (1986) summed up the situation as "static," for better or worse, compared with the early stages of the process. They stated that for additional significant improvements, encounters between moshav and kibbutz children should be brought to the elementary school. They also recommended watching Bustan, the regional school of Kibbutz Maoz Haim that opened that year, to grade 1 children from Beit Yosef and Yardena.

Glazner and Gonen's 1995 Follow-Up Study

Twenty years after Eitan's research and ten years after the Noy-Kostrinsky follow-up, Ettie Gonen and David Glazner conducted another study. The former was principal of the Neveh Eitan school and earlier the Bustan integrative elementary school. The second researcher preceded her as principal at Neveh Eitan. The school itself changed significantly in the decade before the study: There were fewer children in the kibbutz, but the moshav birth rate had dropped also. With the economic and social crisis of the kibbutzim in 1985, the proportion of kibbutz children at the school dropped to 65% in the mid-1990s–246 out of an enrollment of 380; the moshavim, where younger families were having fewer children, had only 40. The other 94 students came from three other sources: 13 from the nearby towns (Beit Shean and Menahemiya), 20 from more distant but relatively prosperous moshavim in the Jordan Valley who preferred the kibbutz-moshav school to closer town schools, and the other 49 were from three groups of Na'aleh[3] adolescents from the former Soviet Union whose parents had sent them to Israel for their secondary education. Most were outstanding students who did not fit in socially in the schools and the kibbutzim where they lived. The changes made for a very heterogeneous school population and improved the position of the children from Beit Yosef and Yardena: They were now admitted individually rather than as a disadvantaged group, there were fewer of them, and far fewer were dropping out–all of which reduced points of social friction. Gonen and Glazner (1995) used a physical law to sum up the changes in the significantly larger school: "A flexible object standing on three to five legs is much more stable than a rigid object standing on two unequal ones."

The dropout rate of the Beit Yosef and Yardena children was examined over 20 years, particularly the number of those graduating from grade 12 with complete or partial matriculation certificates. The dropout rate for moshav children went down significantly–from 61% to 25%–but still presented problems compared to that of the kibbutzim where it had dropped from 19% to 6% because of the increased importance for civilian life of matriculation in the army. Kibbutz and moshav students were balanced, in view of their proportion in the school population, in the group that obtained partial matriculation. Both groups did significantly better in matriculation examinations, but there was still some imbalance with 74% success among students from the kibbutz and only 60% among those from Beit Yosef and Yardena.

Parents, teachers, and graduates were interviewed. (Two women graduates from the moshavim are themselves teaching at Neveh Eitan and at Dekalim.) Gonen and Glazner concluded from the interviews that, after 20 years, integration is regarded as an unqualified success both scholastically and socially, despite difficulties still unsolved and gaps still unbridged. All those interviewed cited the highly significant role of Neveh Eitan teachers in this connection and the fact that the young parents in the moshavim, themselves graduates of Neveh Eitan, can help their children study, which their parents could not do for them. Having been through the situation, they can help their children deal with the social problems of the new school as well.

People from kibbutzim and moshavim testified to openness and rapprochement, both stating that school achievements and the students' extracurricular social and cultural activities benefited from the more heterogeneous school population. Particular mention was made of integration in the last decade beginning in grade 1: Children from Beit Yosef and Yardena have been going to Bustan integrative school with Maoz Haim children since 1986, which amalgamated with Dekalim, the larger school, in 1993. Gonen and Glazner (1995) concurred with the conclusions of previous studies. Like their predecessors, they stressed the importance of a strong, heterogeneous, regional community that supports not only education but also alternative economic projects in view of the difficulties facing agriculture–and leisure programs for adults. These changes based education neither on the ethnic group or the type of settlement that students come from but on a complex, regional mosaic representing Israel's varied populations.

Integration in Dekalim (1986-96)

A year after the last follow-up at Neveh Eitan, Glazner (1996) returned to document integration at Dekalim. This kibbutz-moshav elementary school was the first to take moshav children into grade 1, beginning in 1993. His only sources were written documents, the local press, and interviews with teachers. Glazner (1996) found strong resemblances to other elementary and secondary schools. We focus on the intermediate stages of integration that are the most significant and draw conclusions as to academic and social integration in general.

1977-1987: A School for Three Kibbutzim with 150 Students

Dekalim, the regional elementary school, was established at Kibbutz Hamadia in cooperation with Kfar Ruppin and Neveh Eitan. All three were partners in the Neveh Eitan school, which had two other partners: Maoz Haim and Neveh Ur of Hakibbutz Hameuhad, who favored a school in every kibbutz and retained the smaller, more intimate framework in their local elementary schools. In the early stages, grade 1 of Dekalim remained in the home kibbutz in contrast with grades 2 to 6 where there were only 15 to 20 students in all and sometimes only one or two at each grade level. Ties among the kibbutzim were close, school activities took place at each of the member settlements with the active participation of parents and other members, and the kibbutz *metaplot* (housemothers) were regular visitors to the classrooms.

1981-1986: Outside Requests for Integration at Dekalim Are Not Met

Beginning in 1980, the regional council addressed requests to Dekalim to take in elementary school children from Yardena (and Beit Yosef), which was still suffering from insufficient students and teachers. Until 1984 there was no response from the kibbutzim or the school, which wanted to retain its intimate setting of less than 150 students. In the 1984-1985 school year, the subject was discussed by the kibbutzim and the school administration, which supported integration for the same pragmatic reasons that motivated Neveh Eitan 15 years earlier. Additional reasons arose from the positive experiences at the secondary school: increased academic and social variety and a larger teaching staff. At the same time, the difficulties at Neveh Eitan were cited in opposition to integration: larger, heterogeneous classes, social problems, more students with learning difficulties, and less kibbutz experience in the daily life of the school.

Nonetheless, kibbutz general meetings at both Neveh Eitan and Kfar Ruppin affirmed the decision to integrate, although Hamadia opposed it, particularly in view of difficulties anticipated from having the school in their kibbutz. All partners had to ratify qualitative changes at the school, so the proposal was turned down. Hamadia demanded that a regional body draw up a new map of elementary education that would consider the needs of the moshavim. Such a regional body was established and included representatives of the Ministry of Education. Bustan, a regional elementary school, was established in Maoz Haim in 1986 as a result of the body's recommendation. Their existing school took in some 50 moshav children, giving up the 50-year-old tradition of a school for kibbutz children only. Changes were far greater than merely doubling the school population: The school developed new curricula along with learning centers that also served students having difficulty, created close links with moshav parents, and tried hard to adapt activity-oriented teaching to the needs of the heterogeneous population. Opposition of teachers, parents, and the kibbutz establishment at Maoz Haim was eventually overcome, and the school showed academic and social achievements that won it the Ministry's National Award for Education.

1987: Children from Neveh Ur Join the School

The local kibbutz school was the preferred framework in Hakibbutz Hameuhad, but the Neveh Ur school had only 40 students in the 1980s. Rather than increasing the school size as Maoz Haim had done, Neveh Ur of Hakibbutz Hameuhad joined the regional school. Members of Neveh Ur had difficulty deciding whether it was to be the smaller school, Bustan–whose educational philosophy was closer to theirs but was a 30 minute drive away and was being reorganized–or Dekalim–better established and only half the distance away. Moreover, the perception was that sooner or later Bustan would amalgamate with Dekalim, so Neveh Ur opted for a single change of schools, and it proved to be correct, as Bustan never had more than 120 students. When Neveh Ur joined Dekalim, the school grew to 200 students but was able to retain the same number of classes and the same infrastructure. The

Neveh Ur staff brought its active learning methods to Dekalim, which had by now become a more conventional school. Conflicting styles of teaching and learning slowed down the absorption of Neveh Ur staff and students for more than a year, but success did follow and the present principal is from that kibbutz. When the Neveh Ur school joined Dekalim, it accelerated the awareness that a kibbutz school can no longer remain small. It must grow and become regional, admitting new populations, including those like Beit Yosef and Yardena, just as the Neveh Eitan secondary school, into which Dekalim children graduate, had done earlier.

1989: Children from Moshav Tel Teomim and Immigrant Children

Two years after Neveh Ur, Dekalim and the kibbutz partners in the school were ready for a request from the regional council and parents from Tel Teomim for the school to find place for 12 children in a National–rather than a National Religious–elementary school. The parents, second generation immigrants from Kurdistan, came from moshavim in the southern Beit Shean Valley. Some had gone to the religious kibbutz school in Sdeh Eliahu but as adults did not continue the religious life-style. Once the Ministry of Education and the regional council guaranteed the operating budget and their support for increased class size, the request was met with virtually no opposition. The children encountered scholastic and social difficulties, but because they were few and distributed among several classes, teachers were able to tutor them within the homeroom framework, keeping parents in the picture and carrying out social and cultural activities that eased the absorption process. More so than before, the curriculum emphasized Jewish tradition, home, family and agriculture, so that children from Tel Teomim could contribute to class discussions. Classes grew even larger and more heterogeneous when the children of Russian immigrants from the kibbutzim and moshavim in the area enrolled. With 30% of the students new to Dekalim, teaching became much harder, especially in the upper grades. School staff made a most significant contribution to the absorption of the new groups, with relatively good cooperation from the parents and from the local council of their moshav. While the parents were open to the new school, as those of Yardena and Beit Yosef had been before them, they had difficulty accepting its cultural and social emphases and attached more importance to formal learning achievements. In sum, the school took another step forward on the way to kibbutz-moshav integration, having learned the lessons of the past from

Neveh Eitan, where most Dekalim teachers sent their children and which some had attended themselves in the period when it was an integrative school.

1993-1994: Bustan, the Kibbutz-Moshav School, Unites with Dekalim

In 1993, after admission of the Tel Teomim children, Bustan remained small with an enrollment of only 100 students. The small size was a burden to Maoz Haim teachers and economically was too costly: The kibbutz economy could not handle the costs of providing the unique education for a small number of children, many of whom had learning difficulties. After receiving pressure from the Ministry of Education and the regional council, the kibbutz general meeting decided to join Dekalim after 50 years of running their own school and 7 years of operating Bustan.

The union with Bustan brought 100 new students: 50 from Maoz Haim and 50 from Beit Yosef-Yardena. Dekalim's enrollment now numbered 300. The Bustan staff, used to teaching heterogeneous classes, contributed much to scholastic and social integration at Dekalim. Class size grew to 35 but, in contrast to the past, economic exigencies now made it impossible to divide such a class. The moshav children added to the proportion who had learning difficulties–as high as 30%. Classes were large, heterogeneous, and community-based rivalries developed.

When the Tel Teomim moshav children allied themselves with those moshav children from Beit Yosef and Yardena, the differences between kibbutz and moshav children were exacerbated once again. Social and disciplinary problems developed to the point of violence, like Neveh Eitan in 1972-1973. Having learned from experience there and at Bustan, the staff immediately took a series of parallel actions that solved the problems in the course of the first year. There was class and individual reinforcement so students would learn how to study, with smaller but still heterogeneous learning groups. Visits were made to kibbutzim and moshavim, with emphasis on the special nature of each place. Social activities highlighted the idea of equality in difference, both in the classroom and outside it, and teachers kept up individual contacts with students and moshav parents.

Over these years, and especially since the mid-1990s, certain characteristics of Dekalim have become stronger:

1. The school has a very heterogeneous population, having admitted, besides the groups mentioned above, children from problem fami-

lies from the Kfar Yehezkel residential school. They did this from a sense of educational duty to those different and in difficulty.

2. In the heterogeneous kibbutz-moshav school, socio-cultural differences between those two populations have sharpened around attitudes toward Jewish tradition and to politics. (The national-rightist stance of moshav children and parents generally opposes that of the school staff.) The school tries to cope by means of formal and nonformal multicultural curricula that educate to mutual acquaintance and mutual respect.

3. The union with Bustan brought in more heterogeneous teaching methods as well as experimental projects in individual and group study, in the best tradition of kibbutz education. While not all these electives have succeeded, the school, aware of the need for new and varied methods, devotes considerable resources to developing them.

4. Special education is handled without separating the student from the homeroom class, except for a limited group of children with extraordinary difficulties. Ways have been found for kibbutz teachers, as well as community center staff in the moshavim, to assist the children in their home communities.

5. Large class size has weakened links with the parents. In response, a parents' committee has been set up to maintain direct written and oral contact with the teachers.

6. Cultural relations between kibbutz and moshav children have improved over the years, in part because of school social and cultural activities. Kibbutz residents have better relationships with the children of Beit Yosef and Yardena who, like their parents, have had longer ties with kibbutz children.

7. Graduates of the Dekalim integrative school go on to Neveh Eitan, which adapted to the special conditions of the Beit Shean Valley. The two schools are similar and complement one another, maintaining constant contacts, as Amnon Eitan anticipated in the first days of intermediate division integration in the 1970s. Now integration starts with grade 1. There is no research data on integration at Dekalim, but indications are that despite scholastic and social difficulties, as in the case of Neveh Eitan, one can sum up the decade of integration since Bustan as a success.

DISCUSSION AND CONCLUSION

The history of integration in Beit Shean Valley day schools reveals that three variables played a very clear role in decisions regarding school size: the need to grow for social, economic, and scholastic reasons, making the school more comprehensive, and preserving the relative autonomy of the kibbutzim in school administration. The kibbutzim agreed to changes on condition that they retained this autonomy: Hence the schools are run to this day by kibbutz members. Most school staff personnel are from the kibbutz, although there are many outside teachers. Policy in general is largely determined by the kibbutzim. From the beginning, the moshavim have preferred not to become full partners in the secondary school, mainly for economic reasons. Even if they had become members, there is little doubt that kibbutz autonomy would have been maintained, if only because of their majority of five kibbutzim against two moshavim that eventually combined into one.

Three variables remained, then, in the "size dilemma model." In regard to the two schools, we have seen how important their unique and intimate quality was in educating to kibbutz life in the classroom and in the social life and work that was part of the school experience–features now prized by the school staff. As against these desiderata, besides the pragmatic considerations, there was the integration ideology. In the kibbutz movement, the period after the Six-Day War (1967) was one of reawakening that showed itself mainly in a new wave of settlement, not only on the Golan Heights and in the Jordan Valley, but in Galilee, the Negev, and the Arava within Israel's earlier borders. The kibbutzim assumed true egalitarian integration in their surroundings–after years when the employer-employee relationship was virtually their only tie with their neighbors. Before integration in education, graduates of kibbutz schools contributed to Israeli society as officers in elite military units and as youth leaders during their pre-enlistment community service year. From this point on, kibbutz members and the educators wanted contacts with the rest of Israeli society to begin during the school years, first at the secondary and then in the elementary grades.

"Uniqueness" and "integration" were weighty but contradictory ideological considerations. Nonetheless, a new and candid examination of the principles of kibbutz education when integration began revealed ideological reasons that could stand against those that supported uniqueness. For one thing, kibbutz education was from the outset non-selective, relating to each child according to his ability, thus resembling the integration concept. Besides, kibbutz education supported integration with the community and contributing to Israeli society as a whole, and the regional community had gradually become part of its daily life. Kibbutz education also combined classroom teaching with values education, and through integration kibbutz children were educated to accept others. They were now better able to compare kibbutz life with other life-styles.

The delay in integrating the elementary schools shows that when integration started, uniqueness and integration were equally strong principles. Everyone understood, particularly after the research of Amnon Eitan (1975), that integration had to begin as early as possible. Nonetheless, the desire to preserve the uniqueness of the kibbutz system at least in the elementary school predominated for a full 10 years after integration in the intermediate division at Neveh Eitan. It even prevented Maoz Haim and Neveh Ur from joining Dekalim, the regional kibbutz elementary school. What tipped the ideological scales within the "size dilemma model" were practical regional conditions: Demographic surveys showed numerous departures from the kibbutzim and a falling moshav birth rate. Improved transportation made it possible to extend the school community beyond the immediate surroundings, south to other moshavim and to the towns of Beit Shean and Menahemiya, to the Jordan Valley moshavim, and even to the Kfar Yehezkel residential school. Adapting integration to local conditions made it succeed even against the highly prized uniqueness of education in the kibbutz.

"Local regionalism" enters as a theoretical addition to our conclusions on Beit Shean Valley integration. It does not contradict the integration research quoted briefly earlier in this article, on which Eitan (1975) so largely based his first study, but rather adds a dimension. Eitan called it "neighborhood," the two-way tie between the school and its community. Children go to school relatively near home, and home and community quality help strengthen the school. To this perception of community we add two interrelated dimensions: (a) regionalism, the tie among children from different types of settlement which contributes to integration because it reflects real life in the whole of their society; and (b) localism, in which regionalism has to be adapted to the local conditions of each region. All the integration studies in the Beit Shean Valley agree that such adaptation was a necessary condition for the success of a highly complex educational move. Moreover, we found this dimension very significant in other regions in Israel. This is true for the residential institutions of Hakibbutz Ha'rtzi, which opened to others and to other life-styles in the late 1980s. These residential schools were notably more orthodox in preserving the educational uniqueness of the kibbutz than the day schools were. Nonetheless, they took the path of local regionalism (Dror, 1999).

In conclusion, what lessons of communal and international scope can be learned from the case history of integration in Beit Shean Valley day schools, beyond the certainty that successful integration is a long process that starts at an early age and depends heavily on the educational team?

1. Local regionalism is important for educational integration wherever it is, but especially in remote rural areas. "Community" is a flexibly defined concept that varies with all the components of local geography.
2. Following Miller's model (1980) that summed up integration research in different countries, agreement–even passive agreement within the absorbing community–is an important condition for success. The kibbutzim went from opposing to supporting integration only after members discussed the matter in depth, weighing both pragmatic and ideological considerations. Without this internal clarification process that changed attitudes, true integration would not have been possible.
3. Integration is a difficult and complex process where learning achievements are accompanied by many social difficulties. Prompt, intelligent attention to these can reduce the problems of the future. The Beit Shean Valley regional community was quick to learn from the early failures in Neveh Eitan and to apply the lessons in the integrative elementary schools. The regional learning process parallels those that went on separately inside the individual communities.
4. Multicultural learning was part of integration from its inception. It included the Bar Mitzvah program, exchange of visits, and building new emphases on agriculture and Jewish tradition into the curriculum. Multicultural learning transposes, as it were, elements from the experience of a particular regional community into the local curriculum, running parallel to and complementing the social and cultural activities of the class and of the school as a whole in the interests of integration.
5. The Beit Shean Valley experience indicates that the closer the social and cultural contacts among the adults, the more successfully their children will integrate. In local regionalism, the integration of children whose parents meet outside the school framework will help surmount barriers in both generations. Lifelong education is the appropriate principle for adult learners who are then able to help their children. Cultural activities for adults as well as children and adolescents thus assist integration, expanding the "community school" to include the entire geographical area in which regional schools function, with their communal centers around them.

NOTES

1. A cooperative settlement less collective in organization than the kibbutz.

2. Beit Chinuch is a transliteration of the Hebrew "school home," an institution that offers a long school day and non-formal educational activities along with classroom studies.

3. Hebrew acronym for "Youth Immigrating Before Parents."

REFERENCES

Dror, Y. (1995). School size as a function of uniqueness, autonomy, integration and comprehensiveness: An historical model with current implications. *Journal of Educational Administration and History, 27*(1), 35-50.

Dror, Y. (1999). Reducing totality and expanding the community: "Local regionalism" in the Kibbutz secondary education. In M. Folling-Albers & W. Folling-Albers (Eds.), *The transformation of collective education in the Kibbutz–the end of utopia?* (122-135). Frankfurt: Peter Lang.

Eitan, A. (1975). *On the interaction between Moshav and Kibbutz children in Hativat Habeynaim in Neveh Eitan*. Unpublished master's thesis, Tel-Aviv University, Tel-Aviv, Israel.

Glazner, D. (1996). *The development of the integration in "Dekalim" school–on the combining of Moshav and Kibbutz children in Beit Shean valley*. Jerusalem: School of Education, The Hebrew University. (in Hebrew)

Gonen, E., & Glazner, D. (1995). *The integration in "Neveh Eitan" school–analysis of the state, 1995*. Jerusalem: School of Education, The Hebrew University. (in Hebrew)

Miller, N. (1980). Making school desegregation work. In W. G. Stepan & J. R. Feagin (Eds.), *School desegregation: Past, present and future*. (309-348). New York: Plenum Press.

Niv, A., & Bar-On, D. (1992). *The dilemma of size from a system learning perspective: The case of the kibbutz*. Greenwich, CT: Jay Press, Inc.

Noy, R., & Kostrinski, M. (1986). *Re-checking the integration in "Neveh Eitan" school*. Oranim: The Institute of Improvement of the Ways of Teaching. (in Hebrew)

The Zweig Center for Special Education: School-University Partnership and Professional Development School According to the Heritage of Kibbutz Education

Yuval Dror

SUMMARY. The Zweig Center for Special Education, based on the heritage and history of kibbutz special education, is a model for the school-university partnership and of the professional development school. This model integrates kibbutz education with special education in a unique way.

Kibbutz education is traditionally non-selective, emphasizing an educating society/environment; the integration of educational factors; the integration of society, studies, and work; active learning; informal methods; autonomy in the children's society; and autonomy of educational staff. These make possible schools as laboratories of community partnerships,

The author was Head of Oranim (1990-1997) and a faculty member in the Haifa University division at Oranim from the late 1970s. The special education department is a part of another division of Oranim–the College division–but in order to be objective as a "participant observer," the article is based on documents of the Zweig Center, kept in the archives of Oranim, as well as on general educational research and theory.

With thanks and love to Haddasa Zweig–a wonderful person who really loves people.

[Haworth co-indexing entry note]: "The Zweig Center for Special Education: School-University Partnership and Professional Development School According to the Heritage of Kibbutz Education." Dror, Yuval. Co-published simultaneously in *Child & Youth Services* (The Haworth Press, Inc.) Vol. 22, No. 1/2, 2001, pp. 135-148; and: *Innovative Approaches in Working with Children and Youth: New Lessons from the Kibbutz* (ed: Yuval Dror) The Haworth Press, Inc., 2001, pp. 135-148. Single or multiple copies of this article are available for a fee from The Haworth Document Delivery Service [1-800-342-9678, 9:00 a.m. - 5:00 p.m. (EST). E-mail address: getinfo@haworthpressinc.com].

© 2001 by The Haworth Press, Inc. All rights reserved.

135

training opportunities, and action research that show the varieties of school-university partnership and professional development schools. *[Article copies available for a fee from The Haworth Document Delivery Service: 1-800-342-9678. E-mail address: <getinfo@haworthpressinc.com> Website: <http://www.HaworthPress.com> © 2001 by The Haworth Press, Inc. All rights reserved.]*

KEYWORDS. Kibbutz teachers college, kibbutz special education, School University Partnership, Professional Development School, progressive education, special education

The "Dr. Leon and Haddasa Zweig Center" was established in 1991 at the Oranim Teachers College, The School of Education of the Kibbutz Movement. It is the latest step in the history of kibbutz special education. The Zweig Center in its approach was shaped according to the heritage and principles of kibbutz special education described in this volume, together with the methods of School-University Partnership and Professional Development School mentioned by the Holmes Group (1986; 1995). The lessons for the international community are rooted both in kibbutz education and the innovations of higher education and teacher training. The Zweig Center is an example of the current practices of kibbutz education: openness to the community environment and cooperation between the educational system and its community. These are "the state of art" in education as a whole.

We begin with a short overview of kibbutz special education and the main theoretical terms of the School-University Partnership (SUP) and the Professional Development School (PDS). This is followed by a description of the Zweig Center and an analysis of Zweig's activities combining kibbutz special education and SUP and PDS principles. Then we describe the implications for other programs in Israel and around the world.

A SHORT HISTORY
OF KIBBUTZ SPECIAL EDUCATION

Kibbutz education was (and is) part of the public national education system, but it was managed independently until recently when its innovations were adopted by the State educational system. The first kibbutz school was established in 1921. By the late 1940s there were 105 schools, but none of them for special education. Children with educational difficulties were then called either "backward" or "disturbed" and were not adequately educated. They were generally removed from school–not necessarily by teachers–for tutoring, sent to work when they got older, and for the most part sent away to institutions in the city.

The Hakibbutz Ha'artzi and Hakibbutz Hameuhad movements set up a child guidance clinic in Tel Aviv in 1953, and in 1957 an institution for the learning impaired was established at Veradim (and later a branch of the clinic at Oranim Kibbutz Teachers' College). Special education then relied heavily on psychoanalysis. The model required a special education teacher in every school and a consultant from the movement's education department assigned to each age level. At the end of the 1950s, Oranim added a year's training course for special education teachers along with one day per month of in-service training for teachers from both movements. At Oranim and Haifa University, Dr. Shmuel Nagler did research on kibbutz children and at the end of the 1960s led special education at Oranim to the status of a three-year college course. Dr. Mordecai Kaufman from Hakibbutz Ha'artzi headed the clinics of the two movements for 35 years, adding treatment of the family to individual treatment of the child.

The special education department of the Ihud Hakkibutzim movement was responsible for psychological consultation clinics for children in Tel Aviv and at Ayelet Hashahar in the Upper Galilee. A special education institute, Neveh Tse'elim, was established in 1953, and the "Progressive Education Framework" at Giv'at Haim in 1957 later served the whole movement. The latter's innovation was exposing the pupil to two environments simultaneously. Children were placed in these classes and with foster families in and near Giv'at Haim four days a week. During one mid-week day and another on the weekend the children were in their own children's society and home kibbutz.

In the 1970s, the direction of special education was "the learning center." Here the child with learning difficulties received individual and group help for part of the school day. The Veradim facility closed, and some children were sent to Neveh Ze'elim and Giv'at Haim (and its vocational section, established in 1975). The clinics were placed in many regional councils and gradually adopted integrative treatment, extending their services to the entire kibbutz community. Since the 1980s, the degree of Bachelor in Education in special education can be earned in the two kibbutzim teachers' colleges. Children with learning difficulties are taught in special education classes within the kibbutz school and not only individually at the learning center. A few kibbutz schools also have classes for the deaf and for autistic children, most of whom come from outside the kibbutz. The Zweig Center is located in the academic unit of special education in Oranim and is a part of the trend toward integrative treatment and supports the inclusion of special education in the community.

THE UNIQUE PRINCIPLES
OF KIBBUTZ SPECIAL EDUCATION

Kibbutz special education from its inception was influenced by Israeli public education as well as by the unique system of kibbutz education. The above mentioned history of kibbutz special education will be analyzed according to the seven principles of kibbutz education as a theoretical framework in the discussion of the Zweig Center.

1. The individual and social education of the child and the youth are at the center of kibbutz education for every child until the 12th grade. Except for its formative period (the 1920s till the 1940s), kibbutz education was non-selective forty years before the State of Israel approved the law of special education (1988) that required all schools to integrate individuals with learning and other difficulties. There are relatively many special education classes in kibbutz elementary and secondary schools.
2. An educating society/environment. The kibbutz is an "ideal type" of "community education" rooted in the local and regional area. This feature can be discerned in the location of kibbutz special education institutions within the rural areas along with special schools, guidance clinics, teachers' colleges, etc. It can also be seen through the unique "double community" method of the "Progressive Education Framework" at Giv'at Haim, and from Dr. Kaufman's familial treatment.
3. The integration of educational factors is "built in" at all the kibbutz special education frameworks as in the kibbutz education system as a whole. In addition to the family and the "external" agencies, the special educators are fully involved in the daily life of those in their charge.
4. Integration of society, studies, and work is a natural part of all the different forms of kibbutz special education, including institutions like Giv'at Haim with its "Progressive Education Framework."

5. Active learning, informal methods, and interdisciplinary approaches.
6. Student autonomy in the children's society, based on close and informal relations between participants, is a principle that is used in kibbutz special education as in all the kibbutz schools. While the regular elementary schools practice these methods more than the secondary ones, it is part of all the kibbutz special education institutions and part of the training curriculum in the kibbutz teachers' colleges.

The autonomy of the kibbutz educational staff enabled all these innovations of kibbutz special education, including the creation of new roles and training courses, before they were adopted by the public educational system.

THEORETICAL BACKGROUND: SCHOOL-UNIVERSITY PARTNERSHIP

The term "School-University Partnership" was defined by Sirotnik and Goodlad (1988) as a "planned effort to establish a formal, mutually beneficial, interinstitutional relationship characterized by sufficient commitment to the effective fulfillment of overlapping functions to warrant the inevitable loss of some present control and authority on the part of the institution currently claiming dominant interest" (pp. 25-26). The partnership is intended to facilitate changes in the schools and their districts and to intensify academic research on education. The key variables of the process are mentioned by Sirotnik and Goodlad (1988):

* The extent and nature of the "partnership" as regards all parties of it;
* The "communication" between the education field and academic organizations;
* The "leadership" of both;
* The "renewal" and "accountability" of the schools. (pp. 178-179)

Schwartz (1990) preferred the term "collaboration" and mentioned other variables of a productive partnership between academia and the field:

* A common agenda acknowledged by the major parties;
* A small group of activities;
* Some small-scale beginning activities;
* A large measure of flexibility;

- A desire to learn from mistakes;
- A focus on activities, not machinery;
- Rewards and status for those truly involved;
- A great deal of comfort with ambiguity. (p. 2)

We shall present and analyze school-university partnerships, adding some ideas to the literature mentioned here.

THEORETICAL BACKGROUND:
PROFESSIONAL DEVELOPMENT SCHOOL

The term "Professional Developmental School" (PDS) was defined in the Holmes report of 1986, and again in 1995, as part of "Tomorrow's Schools of Education" (TSE) report. The main idea is school-university partnership via "experimental schools" in the field that will have mutual connections with academia. The Carnegie report (1986) used the term "clinical schools." Goodlad (1990) used a similar metaphor of schools as hospitals. Linda Darling-Hammond (1994) defined PDS as:

> A major aspect of the restructuring movement in education . . . PDSs aim to provide new models of teacher education and development by serving as exemplars of practice, builders of knowledge, and vehicles for communicating professional understandings among teacher educators, novices, and veteran teachers . . . They allow school and university educators to engage jointly in research and rethinking of practice thus creating an opportunity for the profession to expand its knowledge base by putting research into practice–and practice into research. (p. 1)

The SUP and PDS are mutually connected: PDSs are the "School" part in the partnership with the University and higher education (mainly teacher training) as a whole. Kibbutz special education contained some of their features from its beginning.

THE ZWEIG CENTER:
GOALS, METHODS, AND ACTIVITIES

The Zweig Center for the rehabilitation of children with learning disabilities is a model whereby advanced methods are applied in corrective and rehabilitative teaching in special education. It has four main purposes:

1. Rehabilitation of children and adolescents with learning disabilities who came from the regular education system and from special education facilities.
2. Preparation of students in special education in corrective learning for children with learning disabilities.
3. Guidance for qualified teachers in special education and teachers in "regular" classes who have children with learning disabilities using advanced methods of corrective teaching.
4. Guidance for parents of children with learning disabilities.

The center concentrates on corrective teaching in reading and arithmetic, corrective teaching for children of kindergarten age with problems of readiness in learning, and corrective teaching for children with learning disabilities through the use of computers.

Remedial Reading Methodology

It is believed that the child can read when his or her perceptual thinking, language ability, and his social and emotional maturity have reached a suitable level. The reading skills are practiced until they are automatic. The acquisition of reading skills is gained by an eclectic approach. "Reading" in the case of the children is taught without books on the basis of a personal story or the re-creation of a story told to the child. The direction of the story that the child creates is defined by the needs, ability, and motivation of the child. The teachers make it a positive, pleasant, and meaningful experience.

Remedial Mathematical Learning

Remedial arithmetic is based on the cognitive and neuro-psychological processes the child uses in deriving his answers. The teacher assesses the way the child thinks mathematically and the strategies the child uses in carrying out mathematical tasks. The child's program is personalized, and the leading principle is the interaction between comprehending the procedure and the technical skills involved. As the skills in the sequencing of mathematical operations grow, the child is taught conceptual information on which the technical skills are acquired with mathematical insight.

Corrective Teaching of Readiness for Learning

The concept of readiness for learning relates to the progress of the child in kindergarten in coping with the demands of the school. The readiness for learning is a mixture of characteristics needed for learning: ability to think, emotional maturity, ability to concentrate, motivation for learning, and biological maturity. Exact assessment is used in order to match individual programs to the needs and limitations of the child. The assessment provides information on the way the child thinks, on the connection between the perceptual and thinking functions, and on the style of learning in reading, writing, and arithmetic.

Corrective Teaching Through Computers

The Zweig center staff is aware of the considerable potentials of the computer as a tool in teaching special education, toward three specific aims:

- *Visual thinking*. Non-verbal problems are solved by visual thinking with the aid of the computer. Problems require the use of brain (cognitive) processes such as memory, analogous comparison, and creative thinking.
- *Reflective thinking*. The computer reinforces reflective thinking by giving immediate feedback. It allows the child to practice reflective thinking and thus the child can develop a more mature attitude to information and is able to react with more balance and greater care to fresh information.
- *Specific concepts*. The variety of specific computer programs and games allows work on specific concepts such as colors, shapes, mathematical concepts, language enrichment, and programs for reading and writing.

The computer is a tool that supports and compensates the pupil when integrated into the corrective educational system, especially the learning areas where the child is failing. The computer allows repetition as often as needed and gives concentrated exercises in a patient way, offering immediate feedback. Work with the computer is individual and is naturally paced to the individual. By practicing the varied programs, the child can develop independence in thinking which, in turn, gives a feeling of control that improves the self-image of the child. Finally, the personal pace and the discretion in the learning process decrease social pressure.

The Zweig Center "translates" the methods of corrective learning toward the four different populations into six activities.

A Special Education School for Teaching of Children and Adolescents Ages 5 to 16

One hundred ten children are treated at the center. The children study in the framework of the regular school system, in elementary schools, in special technical frameworks within high schools, or in schools of special education. These children do not receive corrective teaching in the centers where they live. Most children come from under-privileged (kibbutz and non-kibbutz) families, and some of them are new immigrants from Ethiopia and the Soviet Union. The children come to the center twice a week and receive four hours of corrective teaching in every meeting. The teaching is done by Oranim students of special education who are guided by a staff of experts from all four areas mentioned above and a clinical educational psychologist who leads the whole center. The experts and the students are in contact with the families of the children and with the educational system in which the children are studying. They also help the regular teachers of the children to apply the methods of the center in the school.

Pre-Service and In-Service Training

This is for both kibbutz and non-kibbutz populations in the north of Israel. More than 50 students in the third and fourth year of their studies in special education receive training in various therapeutic methods through participation in therapeutic workshops. The workshops are led by psychotherapists, psychologists, counselors, clinical social workers, and teachers of movement therapy. In the years previous to these they were given a foundation in theoretical courses based on the various therapeutic methods. The center also serves teachers of special education who are interested in widening their knowledge and in acquiring new methods of corrective teaching. In addition, teachers can become acquainted with up-to-date professional literature and with new teaching devices. They can also consult and receive guidance from the Center's experts.

Resource and Pedagogic Unit

The relatively "old" pedagogic center has been broadened and re-shaped with:

- New pedagogic games, didactic materials, books, and up-to-date articles;
- Equipment and games to treat sensory-motor difficulties;
- Equipment for "self-service" games: The students and teachers of special education can create materials and games of their own aimed at their unique pupils;
- Expansion of the consultation program given by experts in reading, arithmetic, and readiness for learning to one-day-a-week at Oranim for teachers of special education from the "field."

Computer and Audio-Visual Unit

This is an integral part of the remedial program and located near the resource unit. It includes a computer with a special reading skills program for the severely handicapped and computers with various programs for remedial exercises and enrichment. These aids enable the students and teachers of special education to practice the use of computers in order to apply it in the field in their everyday work. Computer specialists are available in the same method of the resource unit. Audio tapes, video tapes and video, a VCR, and television sets for special education audio-visual materials are also included.

Diagnostic Unit and Practitioners Training Program

The center serves the needs of the "field" for diagnostic services in two ways:

1. Professional diagnostic services at a reasonable fee for children with special needs from the entire northern part of the country (both kibbutz and non-kibbutz born and especially youth from lower socio-economic backgrounds as well as from minority groups). The fee is considerably less than that of the private sector, and the service is more professional and reliable. The unit uses the Learning Potential Assessment Device (LPAD) developed by Reuven Feuerstein of Bar-Ilan University. These holistic diagnoses of reading, writing, arithmetic, and skills of thinking and learning fit the policy of the

Zweig Center. The process includes not only diagnosis but also an intervention program with guidance and evaluation over the long run. This entire process is learned by the graduates of the diagnostic training program, who are teachers with a rich experience in the field of special education.

2. The diagnostic Practitioners Training Program is given one day a week for two years of course study and practice. The LPAD tests are practiced in the unit during the second year of the program under the supervision of educational psychologists and diagnostic specialists. The outstanding graduates are employed by the diagnostic unit after their practice duties in their second year of training.

Research

There are research activities in the center carried out by the staff and the students in the pre-service and in-service training programs. "Action research" as well as other qualitative and quantitative methods are used in these studies. The topics are research into methods of corrective teaching, research into various populations of the children of the center, and research into student and teacher training.

CONCLUSION

1. The Zweig Center is an integral part of the department of special education at the Oranim Teachers College, one of the two kibbutzim teachers colleges in Israel. As such, all its training programs are based on the kibbutz principle of non-selective education for every individual.

2. The Zweig Center serves kibbutz and non-kibbutz populations. It had applied some traditions of "School University Partnership" (Sirotnik & Goodlad, 1988) and "Collaboration" (Swartz, 1990) from the history of kibbutz education (and special kibbutz education in particular) and used them for the benefit of the populations in the area of the kibbutz. Kibbutz education (and society as a whole) is a social and educational laboratory for the external society in Israel and abroad. The Zweig Center disseminated this laboratory to non-kibbutz teachers, researchers, teaching students, and pupils. This was the idea of the Kibbutzim Teachers Colleges in Tel Aviv and Oranim since their establishment in 1939. In the

1940s and 1950s the target populations were kibbutz members as well as *Histadrut* (labor movement) members and their children. From the 1960s onwards the Colleges, located in non-kibbutz surroundings, served the general Israeli population in Tel Aviv and in the north. The educating society/environment is one of the main principles of kibbutz education; the mutual connections of the Zweig Center with its surrounding communities are very unique.

3. The Zweig Center is a very real and intensive laboratory of special education for Oranim: Teachers, researchers, and students. Those who are involved can test their theories and be part of them "on line." The Zweig Center deals with pre-service and in-service training, and by this mixture of populations it prepares all professionals who will work in the field of special education aided by the guidance of Oranim specialists in this area. Every year it serves a new group of 110 pupils and their parents in the diagnostic center. The "integration of educational factors" was and still is a basic feature of kibbutz education. It tries to fit the comprehensive way of kibbutz life to the "totality" of its education.

4. The "Professional Development School" (Darling-Hammond, 1994; Holmes Group, 1995) of the Zweig Center is located two days in a week in the College, based on schools in which Oranim students have their practical training. Having better facilities at Oranim, the "field" comes to "academia," but there are also mutual visits at the schools themselves. This is part of a long tradition of "experimental schools" and kindergartens in Oranim as part of the College service to the community in Haifa and the north of Israel. This is a special way of integrating the teaching students' and pupils' societies, studies, and work in Oranim according to the old kibbutz education principle.

5. The Zweig Center is based on the varied educational media of the experimental school, pre-service and in-service teacher training, resource unit, audio-visual unit, diagnostic unit, and research activities. The services for the field support each other, and the users can find solutions to their problems in one professional place. The impact of special education methods spreads from this unit to the large community of Oranim itself. This "pull of sources/services" was from the very beginning of kibbutz education (and special education, as mentioned in the historical background) a unique feature that strengthened its impact, emphasizing the principle of varied active, informal, and interdisciplinary methods. The kibbutzim teachers colleges used these comprehensive methods since the 1940s.

6. The student autonomy principle in the kibbutz children's societies
    is translated in the Zweig Center in a broader way to close and in-
    formal relations between all the participants and their communi-
    ties: the academic staff and the teaching students, the teaching
    students and the pupils, the teachers and the parents of the 110 pu-
    pils who are served every year by Oranim.
7. The Zweig Center identified the need for a new profession: teachers
    who diagnose the special needs of the pupils in their school. The
    diagnostic center trains these new professionals. In the history of
    kibbutz special education the creation of a new role in the teachers
    colleges–as a response to the needs of the field–occurred twice in
    earlier periods. The role of "special educators" was the profes-
    sional solution of the kibbutz movement to the special needs of
    their relatively small and isolated schools.

LESSONS FOR THE INTERNATIONAL COMMUNITY

The international lessons that can be drawn from Zweig Center at
Oranim are a mixture of principles of the kibbutz special education,
PDS, and SUP. They are relevant to education as a whole.

1. The principle of non-selective individual and social education for
    all the children and the youth must be applied in systems of special
    education everywhere.
2. "Laboratory" communities, not only communal/cooperative ones,
    can be spread in wider surroundings–like the communities in the
    north of Israel in the case of Oranim. This can be the contribution
    of the "field" to academia in their mutual partnership, enabling a
    better "School University Partnership" (Sirotnik & Goodlad,
    1988) and "Collaboration" (Swartz, 1990).
3. "The integration of educational factors," the concern of the popu-
    lations of educators and educated within the academic institution
    and outside it, will strengthen the impact of any educational act. It
    is a basic principle for academia, for the field, and for their part-
    nership.
4. The PDS (Darling-Hammond, 1994; Holmes Group, 1995) can be
    arranged in different ways–and not only in the field itself–so as to
    react to the unique circumstances of the school of education or
    teachers college in its particular location. The "alive" laboratory

school in the academic institution can be the best vehicle for a real partnership between academia and "the field."
5. "Pull of sources/services" and varied active, informal, and inter-disciplinary methods are the right ways for academia to assist the field in their partnership.
6. The communities of lecturers and students in the departments of special education at the academic institutions and the teachers, pupils, and parents of the special education schools must communicate together in close and informal ways.
7. Academia has to identify the new roles that are needed in the field and prepare professional training for it. This partnership, enabled by the autonomy of the professional staff, will mix in an appropriate way the better academic skills of the academia with the better practical experience of the field.

AUTHOR NOTE

Yuvol Dror is Associate Professor in the School of Education, Tel-Aviv University. He was Senior Lecturer and Head of Oranim, The School of Education of the kibbutz movement and Haifa University. His areas of specialization are the history of education (and social-moral education) in Eretz-Israel (pre-statehood) under the British Mandate, progressive education (including kibbutz education), and the development of special methodology in the history of education.

REFERENCES

Carnegie Forum on Education and the Economy. (1986). *A nation prepared: Teachers for the 21st century.* New York: Author.

Darling-Hammond, L. (Ed.). (1994). *Professional Development Schools: Schools for developing a profession.* New York and London: Teachers College Press.

Goodlad, J. I. (1990). *Teachers for our nation's schools.* San Francisco and Oxford: Jossey-Bass.

Holmes Group. (1986). *Tomorrow's schools: A report of the Holmes Group.* East Lansing, MI: Author.

Holmes Group. (1995). *Tomorrow's schools of education (TSE): A report of the Holmes Group.* East Lansing, MI: Author.

Sirotnik, K. A., & Goodlad, J. A. (Eds.). (1988). *School-University Partnership in action: Concepts, cases and concerns.* New York and London: Teachers College Press.

Swartz, H. S. (Ed.). (1990). *Collaboration: Building common agendas.* Washington, DC: Clearinghouse on Teacher Education and American Association of Colleges for Teacher Education.

Index

Absorption, of youth
  Friedben Scale of, 96-97,111-112
  in kibbutz, 40,42,81-83
    collective elements for, 83-87
    individual elements for, 87-89
    policy principles for, 78-79
    school arrangements for, 79-81,
      83
    successes and difficulties of,
      48-50,76-77,89-90
  in Na'aleh Program, 95-108
  as new students, 3-4,12,18
  in secondary schools, 4,40,75-90
Academia field, collaboration on
      special education, 144,
      146-148
Academic achievement
  in regional schools, 120-122
  student absorption and, 81,87-88
Academic courses/programs
  of Kfar Tikva, 31-32
  for kibbutz youth, 55-57,81
  whole school, 2
Academic integration. *See* Educational
      integration
Active learning, in kibbutz model, 2,
      139
Adaptation, of immigrant students
  emotional, 102
  Friedben scale of, 96-97,109-110
  in Na'aleh Program, 95-108
Admission examinations, student
      absorption and, 80-81
Adoption. *See also* Foster families
  motivation for, 41-42,49
  symbolic kibbutz, 56-57
Agricultural community, kibbutz youth
      groups as, 61-62

Alienation, in Russian kibbutz
      students, 93,98,107
Aliyah, making of
  Jewish, through kibbutz youth
      groups, 56,59-60,62-63
  by Russian students, 97
Altruistic giving, 18
Analysis schemes
  for kibbutz education, 1, 5
  for kibbutz youth group,
      58-59,64,71
  for special education, 145-146
Anne Frank Haven, as integration
      model, 4,78-79,83,85-88
Arab communities, kibbutz youth
      group and, 59,61
Arithmetic, corrective teaching of,
      141-142
Army service, by kibbutz children,
      40,50
Attention disorders, in special
      education students, 11,16
Audio-visual aids, for corrective
      teaching, 144,146
Autonomy, in kibbutz education
      model, 2-3,78
  for learning impaired students, 135,
      139,143,147
  as regionalization factor, 117-118,
      117t,130

Bar Mitzvah program, educational
      integration of, 80,122,132
Behavioral problems, in special
      education students, 9,11,16
Beit Hinuch Secondary School,
      regionalization of

Learning Potential Assessment
Device (LPAD), for special
education, 144-145
Learning problems
foster families coping with, 43
in regional schools, 120-122
Learning readiness, corrective
teaching of, 142
Least restrictive environment,
limitations of, 23,25
Liberty, of special needs students,
24-25
Local-regionalism, in kibbutz
regionalization, 117-118,
117t,122,131-132
Love, unconditional, from educators,
39-40
LPAD (Learning Potential
Assessment Device), for
special education, 144-145

Mainstreaming, limitations of, 23,25
Mathematics, corrective teaching of,
141-142
Matriculation examinations
regional schools' impact on, 124
student absorption and, 81,87-88
Mekasheret, for disabled children, 8
Mememiot, for disabled children, 8
Milieu therapy, in special education,
7
Moshavim
regionalization of, 114-115
at Neveh Eitan, 118-129
youth absorption in, 3
Moslem countries, kibbutz youth
group and, 59,64
Motivations
of foster families, 41-42
of students, 43,50
immigrant, 97-100
Multiculturalism, in regional schools,
119-122,124-125,129,132

Na'aleh Program
basis of, 4,93-96
kibbutz affiliation of
adaptation difficulties with,
102-106
integration achievements with,
101-102
non-kibbutz schools *versus,*
100-101, 106
student adjustment with, 95-100
student adjustment in
Friedben scales for, 96-97,
109-112
in kibbutz schools, 95-101
in secular *versus* religious
schools, 100-101,106,108
student participation factors, 97-100
student responses to
assuming Israeli identity, 93,97;
99,102,106,112
conclusions about, 106-108
coping problems, 93,97-98,
100-103,106,111
interpersonal conflict, 93,97-98,
102-104,110
motivational, 97-100
personal distress, 93,97-99,
102-103,109
satisfaction with Israel, 93,97-106,
111
school difficulties, 93,97-98,100,
103-104,110
social acceptance, 93,97-98,
100-102,104,109-110
willingness to settle in Israel, 93,
97,99,101,106,111-112
National values
absorption process for youth, 83-85,
87
kibbutz movement and, 64, 69-71
Nazi persecution, saving youth from, 56,
59-61
Neurological disorders, special
education for, 8-9,11,13,16

Neveh Eitan, regional schools in. *See*
Beit Hinuch Secondary
School
Neveh Ur kibbutz, regionalization of,
126-127
New education. *See* Progressive
education
Non-kibbutz societies
educational learning by, 1-2
integration of, 4-5
in day schools, 4,113-133
in Na'aleh Program,
106,100-101
in Special Education Development School, 4,135-148
Israeli children, education in, 38-39,
41-46
Non-selective principle, of kibbutz
education, 1-2,135,138,
145,147
Normalization
limitations of, 23,25-26,32
principles of, 26-27
Norms. *See* Cultural values
Noy-Kostrinsky study (1986), of
school regionalization,
122-123

Open society, kibbutz as, 49,56,62-64
Oranim Teachers College, special
education program of. *See*
Zweig Center for Special
Education
"Others," kibbutz youth groups as, 56,
62-64,68,70

Palestine, kibbutz youth groups and,
58,60,62
Parents
educators as, 39,56-57,64
kibbutz students' ties with, 83
kibbutz youth groups and

absence of, 56-57,59-64
presence of, 64-66,69-71
regional schools' ties with, 129
youth immigrating without
Jewish, 56-57,59-64
Russian, 94-96
Partnership, as kibbutz ideology, 84-85
PDS. *See* Professional Development
School
Pedagogy, for corrective teaching, 144
Peer groups
integration influence of
as negative, 104-105
as positive, 76,84-85
learning disabled students and,
17-18
Personal problems, foster families
coping with, 43-44
Pioneers, of kibbutz movement, 61,
63-65
changing image of, 66-67,70
Policy, educational, for integrated
programs, 78-79
Politics, of kibbutz movement, 60-65,
69,71,129
Power, of kibbutz movement, 60-65
Practitioners Training Program, for
special education, 144-145
Pre-service training, by Zweig Center
for Special Education, 143,
146
Primary schools, integration of, 37-40
Privatization, kibbutz and, 49
Problem solving, kibbutz and, 49
Problems
personal, foster families coping
with, 43-44
with school. *See* School difficulties
Professional Development School
(PDS)
in international community,
147-148
for special education, 4,136-137,
140
Zweig Center as, 140-146